An Ecumenical Light on
THE RENEWAL OF
RELIGIOUS COMMUNITY LIFE

Taizé

"A community is not created once and for all at its beginning. The only thing that can prevent a community from becoming static or regressive is its daily renewed re-creation." Roger Schutz, *L'Unanimité dans le pluralisme*, p. 34.

"Nor should we forget that anything wrought by the grace of the Holy Spirit in the hearts of our separated brethren can contribute to our own edification." Vatican Council II, *Decree on Ecumenism*, no. 4.

Imprimatur
✠ J. Bluyssen
Buscoduci, 1 dec. 1966

DUQUESNE STUDIES
Theological Series
7

AN ECUMENICAL LIGHT

on

The Renewal of Religious Community Life

Taizé

by
John Heijke, C.S. Sp.

DUQUESNE UNIVERSITY PRESS,
PITTSBURGH, PA.

Editions E. Nauwelaerts, Louvain

DUQUESNE STUDIES

Theological Series

Henry J. Koren, C.S.Sp., S.T.D., editor

Volume One—*Albert Dondeyne*, FAITH AND THE WORLD. xi and 324 pages. Second impression. $5.00

Volume Two—*Peter Schoonenberg, S.J.*, GOD'S WORLD IN THE MAKING. ix and 207 pages. Second impression. $3.95

Volume Three—*Leonard J. Swidler, editor*, SCRIPTURE AND ECUMENISM. vii and 197 pages. $4.95

Volume Four—*William H. van de Pol*, ANGLICANISM IN ECUMENICAL PERSPECTIVE. v and 293 pages. $6.75

Volume Five—*John H. Walgrave, O.P.*, PERSON AND SOCIETY. 182 pages. $4.25

Volume Six—*Bertrand van Bilsen, O.F.M.*, THE CHANGING CHURCH. 433 pages. $7.95

Volume Seven—*John Heijke, C.S.SP.*, AN ECUMENICAL LIGHT ON THE RENEWAL OF RELIGIOUS COMMUNITY LIFE. TAIZÉ. 212 pages. $4.50

Library of Congress Catalog Card Number 67-15785
© 1967, by Duquesne University
Printed in the United States of America

ACKNOWLEDGMENTS

The author and publisher gratefully acknowledge permission to quote from the following works:

Doubleday & Co., New York, Meriol Trevor, *Newman: Light in Winter*, 1963.

Les Editions du Cerf, Paris, *Fêtes et Saisons*, January, 1965, issue.

Harper and Brothers, New York, Walter Lowrie, *Kierkegaard*, 1962.

Helicon, Baltimore, Roger Schutz, *Living Today for God*. English translation copyright © 1962.

Herder and Herder, New York, Max Thurian, *Mary, Mother of the Lord, Figure of the Church*, 1963 (British edition, The Faith Press, Ltd., London). *Unity Man's Tomorrow*, 1962.

Kunstverlag Maria Laach, Maria Laach, *Laacher Hefte*, XXII, 1958.

Longmans, Green and Co., Harlow, Essex, Roger Lloyd, *An Adventure in Discipleship*, 1955.

Panorama chrétien, Paris, interview by Sammy Chabrillan, July, 1963.

Les Presses de Taizé, Taizé, *The Rule of Taizé and Spiritual Directives Following the Rule*, 1965; *Office de Taizé*, 1964; *Aujourd'hui, Journal de Taizé*, various articles; Roger Schutz, *Dynamique de provisoire*, 1965; Roger Schutz, *L'Unanimité dans le pluralisme*, 1966; *Verbum Caro*, various articles.

Quell-Verlag, Stuttgart, Lydia Präger, ed., *Frei für Gott und die Menschen*, 1959.

SCM Press, London, Max Thurian, *Marriage and Celibacy*, 1959; A. M. Allchin, *The Silent Rebellion*, 1958.

PREFACE

THE COMMUNITY OF TAIZÉ is a famous Protestant monastery in which today's tension between Church and world is experienced and "lived" in a unique and inspiring way.

A study of Taizé is of particular importance for the renewal of religious community life because it can present numerous points on which Taizé's refreshing and evangelical view of God's call and man's response in Christ can be of assistance in bringing about the desired "updating" of Catholic monasteries and convents.

At my first visit to Taizé in the Pentecost week of 1959, I entered the village church while the Community was singing the Office. The first words that struck my ears were the scriptural verse: "These men are not drunk, as you suppose . . . , but this is what was spoken of by the prophet Joel: 'And in the last days it shall be, God declares, that I will pour out my Spirit upon all flesh'" (Acts 2:15).

These men are not drunk! Their ideas and deeds are not those of madmen or fanatics, but bear witness to an inspiring sobermindedness in following the Gospel. Studying the story of Taizé and analyzing the Brothers' community life, as it manifests itself in their actions and writings, I would like to draw the attention of all sincere Christians to the evangelical driving force animating this Community and the latter's suggestive ecumenical competence.

John Heijke, C.S.Sp.

TABLE OF CONTENTS

PART FOUR
PRAYER AND WORSHIP

INTRODUCTION

THE CATHOLIC CHURCH contains many varia-
tions of life according to the Evangelical counsels. The
so-called religious state unfolds itself in ever new patterns adjusting to new situations, and often it is difficult
to distinguish the form of these patterns from their content. Nevertheless, we are permitted to say that whatever
discoveries are made with respect to these new patterns
of religious life, they do not refer primarily to the
evangelical counsels themselves but rather to the form
in which the religious state of life, as universally known
and accepted in the Church, finds expression in our time.

For the older religious institutes, these multiform and
ever renewed attempts of adaptation contain an eloquent
and welcome warning: they must ceaselessly keep watch
over their own interior mobility; they must be on guard
to discern any symptoms of hardening and be ready to
counteract the forces that foster a process of calcifi-
cation. For any form of life always bears within itself
the seed of its own degeneration, its own senility.

Our time is privileged in being able to witness something more profound than merely new forms of a religious state that is generally accepted in the Church. We
are fortunate enough to witness the discovery of the very
practice of monastic life, the birth of the first stage of
cenobitic or community life itself. We can witness this
birth within our Christian world, in an ecclesial community that has not possessed a single form of monastic
life for centuries, viz., Reformational Christianity. The
tradition of this ecclesial community has been able to

begin "with a clean slate," to use an expression of one of
the founders of this Reformational monastic way of life.[1]

Within the world of Reformational Christianity it was
not simply a matter of discovering a new form of the
religious state, but the very viability of the evangelical
counsels was the question. Thus we are offered here an
opportunity to look at community life at a stage of development in which it is brand-new and not yet covered with
the unavoidable incrustation of centuries. Within the
Catholic Church we have had, and continue to have, our
debates concerning the timeliness of celibacy, of a life of
obedience under authority, of a life-long commitment in
a religious community. But here, in the Reformational
Church, comes an unexpected, and in any case unsus-
pected, witness in favor of such a life.

The elan, the inventive and enterprising spirit, the
youthful dynamism of these fresh Protestant communities may be disturbing the repose and lethargy of some
Catholic religious communities. They may constitute an
unintentional question mark in regard to anxiously preserved practices now unmasked as sterile, wholly anti-
quated and inauthentic. On the other hand, however, these
Protestant religious communities are an inspiring source
of encouragement for all those who believe in the value of
religious community life, for those who try to preserve
and renew their confidence in God's promises (Mk.
10:29-30), in spite of all disillusionments.

The presence of those youthful communities in a
Christian world in which the different Churches have left
their spiritual ghettos and in which the life of each lies
revealed to the gaze of all, rouses our consciousness and,
at the same time, fills us with courage. While the exist-

1. Roger Schutz, "Die Entstehung von Kommunitäten in den
Kirchen der Reformation," *Frei für Gott und die Menschen*, Stuttgart, 1959, p. 43.

ence of such communities undermines established certainties, it confirms again the viability of an ideal that had begun to lose some of its lustre.

That is why we humbly but gratefully accept the description of the essentials of religious community life offered to us by the Brothers of Taizé—a description which contains, at the same time, the results of the experiences and the spiritual voyage of exploration of this community itself. We accept it gratefully, not as a belated recognition that we were right or as a confirmation of an evangelical truth which we have been preaching for a long time. We humbly acknowledge that there is no reason for us to shout victory. The picture unfolded by Taizé does not present something that lies behind us, but is a vision of the future, of our future. It does not recall our point of view but projects our task before us.

PART ONE

THE RELIGIOUS COMMUNITY
OF TAIZÉ: ITS BACKGROUND
AND HISTORY

CHAPTER ONE

THE BACKGROUND

1. *The Importance of the Anglican Communities*

THE INITIATIVE to re-introduce religious community life into the Reformational world arose among Anglo-Saxon Christians. In the past decade enormous publicity has been given to all kinds of experiments concerned with the re-introduction of religious life in the world of the Reformation. This publicity could easily create the impression that the revival of community life is solely and entirely due to German and French initiatives around the years of World War II; it could make us forget that Anglican religious communities outdate them by a century.

We are not concerned here with the rather useless question of who was first. Our time has seen the huge growth of international travel and, in particular, more intense and constantly increasing interdenominational contacts; these factors alone suffice to justify the suspicion that the Reformational religious communities on the European continent were not born without being influenced by the Anglican form of religious life. However, even if in a particular case there was no question of any conscious osmosis, it would be useful to be acquainted with that century of "prehistory." For the historical perspective offered by the Anglican communities makes it possible for us to recognize certain features and tendencies of the new Reformational communities and to evaluate them more easily. That perspective also seems to disclose a certain, perhaps unintended, affinity between the function of these Anglican communities in their Church and the more recent monastic life within the Reformational world of today and tomorrow.

The communities that arose in the nineteenth century Church of England owed their birth to the inspiration provided by prominent leaders of the Oxford Movement. The desire to lead a holy life was one of the driving forces of the Oxford Movement, and this desire for a more intense Christian life was accompanied by great knowledge of theology and of history. The Tractarians were seized by an elan, but enlightened by their great interest and knowledge of Patristic Christianity. They rediscovered the value of monasticism in the old Church, and this rediscovery was accompanied by an ever-increasing inner dissatisfaction with the bourgeois establishment of a State Christendom.

Nothing, so they thought, could contribute more to a renewal of Christian life than intensified prayer and a restoration of sacramental life. True, men like John Henry Newman as well as the first sisterhoods themselves were not blind to the fact that a new era was coming, an era with social needs that appealed with an ever increasing force to the Christian conscience. We may even say that the first sisterhoods ultimately owed their "credentials" among their contemporaries and fellow-believers to their concern with their fellow-men. Nevertheless, it remains true that their vocation lay primarily in the realm of liturgical and sacramental restoration.

A first step in the direction of the rebirth of the Anglican religious community life was the fact that the leaders of the Oxford Movement gradually began again to value the practice of prayer at fixed times, that is, the Office. But they were even more concerned with the restoration of sacramental life that had suffered an eclipse. In the religious community foundations which they inspired, this life began again to develop. Frequent Holy Communion, regular reception of the sacrament of Penance and a sense for the liturgy—all this could again develop after 1845 in the religious sisterhoods. These communities of Christians which, despite all their diversities, unanimously endeavored to give greater depth to life provided the Tractarians with a suitable medium within the Church for experiments. These communities became, as it were, the laboratories of the Anglican Church's revival in nineteenth century England. In these small and flexible groups revival ideas could be tested for their value and viability before they were introduced to the Church community at large. In them the Christian convictions and principles of life could be experimented with and given an existential form. Conversely, the sisterhoods exercised a fertile influence on the orientation of thought and Christian vision of the Tractarians. In these communities of "available" Christians, dogmatic truth also became perceptible again in aspects that had hitherto remained concealed.

Since then there have been many occasions in which one could observe that kind of interconnection between, on the one hand, the communal experiment and, on the other, a deepening and a renewal of man's understanding of dogma. It is not too far-fetched to claim that this phenomenon is perceived not only by suspicious or enthusiastic outside observers, but also and even primarily by the members of such communities and that it is experienced by them as a surprise, an event that is at the same time both uprooting and enriching. Perhaps this challenging event is related to the *"dépassement,"* the self-transcendence to which the community of Taizé so often and so insistently invites both its members and others.

In the Anglican sisterhoods, the ideas and aspirations of the Tractarians were able to maintain and develop themselves, in spite of the fact that for a long time the Tractarians led a life marked by suspicion and isolation. Those communities functioned as a kind of spiritual "reservations" fostering and preserving the catholic impulse for the Church of England until this impulse could be communicated to the Church at large through the subsequent foundation of male religious communities and their pastoral work.

It was fortunate that the bond between these communities and their own Church remained, generally speaking, intact; neither side broke it. For it has frequently happened that valuable and inspiring trends of Christian life ended by splitting a Church because the latter left no room to form small, sensitive and flexible communities. Instead of acting in a renewing and broadening way within the ecclesial community at large, thereby making it more catholic, more universal, these seeds of new life had to develop outside the bosom of their mother Church. Their secession obviously contributed to making life within that Church more one-sided, more narrow-minded and more rigid, for a revitalizing influence was thus prevented from acting beneficially upon that life. For the leaders of the Oxford Movement, Methodism provided the classical example. As Newman wrote in his essay about Demetrias:

> St. Augustine's monasteries were intended as the refuge of piety and holiness, when the increasing spread of religion made Christians more secular. And we may confidently pronounce that such provisions, in one

shape or other, will always be attempted by the more serious and anxious part of the community, whenever Christianity is generally professed. In Protestant countries, where monastic orders are unknown, men run into separatism with this object. Methodism has carried off many a man who was sincerely attached to the Established Church, merely because that Church will admit nothing but what it considers "rational" and "sensible" in religion.[1]

In the same sense Pusey pointed to the ecumenical function of religious communities within the Church:

The Church of England should be large enough to contain every soul who would, with devoted heart, labour for her. We mourn now that Wesley was not led to form an order within the Church, rather than rend those thousands upon thousands from her. We mourn here the loss of deep devoted fealty, of strong intellectual energy, of clear-sighted faith, of ardent piety, lost to us.[2]

In many respects the nineteenth century Anglican communities were pioneers. A great spirit of initiative was needed to undertake the re-introduction of religious community life in a place where it had been taboo for several centuries. Yet these communities managed to break through this taboo and wished to make themselves available for a "holy experiment." In this way they have contributed greatly to the metamorphosis which the Church of England has undergone since 1840. And they have undoubtedly exercised an enormous influence that was both deepening and ecumenical. (These two aspects generally go together.)

1. John Henry Newman, *Historical Sketches. The Church of the Fathers,* London, 1873, p. 165.
2. Remark made during the Church Congress of 1862 at Oxford; quoted by A. M. Allchin, *The Silent Rebellion. Anglican Communities 1845-1900,* London, 1958, p. 141.

Thus it would be wrong to say that the originators of these communities suffered from a lack of imagination when one notes that the Anglican religious community life did not assume the many forms now manifested by its Protestant counterpart. The renewal undertaken with so much courage by the Oxford Movement leaders put a strong emphasis on restoration. They were greatly concerned with manifesting and underscoring the unbroken continuity of the Anglican Church—and of their own tendencies within that Church—with the pre-Reformation Church. Over and beyond the far-reaching reform of the Church in the sixteenth century, they carefully endeavored to restore the form of the undivided pre-Reformational Church in England.

This very attempt, however, is one of the reasons why a Catholic is disappointed in his expectations when he hopes to find today in the Anglican communities forms of religious life that remain unexplored within his own Church. He is grateful to find there familiar forms, sometimes even more strict, more punctual and more radical than the ones he is accustomed to. Nevertheless, his imagination does not find there any food for thought, any opportunity to take a fresh look at things that are familiar to him, any chance to discover hidden or overlooked potentialities. He does not find an old ideal in a refreshingly new form, but the same familar pattern of life in the same familiar terms. Visiting those communities, he experiences at once a feeling of solidarity; he looks, as it were, in a mirror.

In these communities also the original mobility has yielded to the rather static stability of the institutional. The period of "experiment" is past, and the provisional has given way to the established way of doing things. The male Anglican communities are mainly institutes of priests. Even in the Benedictine Abbey of Nashdom, non-priests are only an unimportant part of the community. The clerical element has gained the upperhand there also with the result that there is less room for the many forms life in common could otherwise assume. The Anglican convents of sisters generally have a rather strict rule of closure; thus they also answer the question of the relationship between Church and world in a one-sided way although this answer is not without value. The religious garb establishes an undeniable and permanent dividing line between the members of a community and the members of the Church at large; and thus, in spite of the community's service to the Church, suggests an unmistakable aloofness whose value today is no longer unquestionable.

2. *The Recent Revival of Religious Community Life in the World of the Reformation*

It is no pure coincidence that the rediscovery and revaluation of religious community life in the contemporary Protestant world is a phenomenon which simultaneously manifested itself in several places within Reformational Christianity. Taizé, Grandchamp, the Sisters of Mary (*Marienschwestern*) of Darmstadt and the Brotherhood of Christ (*Christusbrüderschaft*) of Selbitz; all are foundations that arose around World War II.[3] They all originated in more or less the same Church-historical situation; and, in general, they were received in the world of the Reformation with fairly great openness, even though that openness was not always immediately evident. These

3. For the Darmstadt sisterhood see Mutter M. Basilea Schlink, *Oekumenische Marienschwesternschaft*, Darmstadt-Eberstadt, 1961; for the Selbitz brotherhood see Hanna Hümmer, *Gott ruft dem, was nicht ist, dasz es sei. Ein Bericht vom Werden und Werk der Christusbruderschaft in Selbitz*, Selbitz, Oberfranken, n.d.

facts cannot be ascribed to a mutually pre-arranged
agreement and even less to a purely coincidental set of
circumstances. On the contrary, they are connected with
other phenomena in the Church which, together, constitute the Church-historical character of the post-war era
and which undoubtedly make these decades a turning
point in the history of the Church.

In spite of the fact that progressively more people cut
their ties with the Church, the past decades have wit-
nessed a renewed interest of the Reformational world in
the norms and bonds of Church life. There exist not only
a more intense and more developed life of liturgical worship but also a greater appreciation for a doctrinal norm
within one's confession of faith. After the liberal theology
of the nineteenth and early twentieth centuries, the tide
has turned in liberal-minded Christianity. Although such
terms as "fundamentalist," "orthodox," "free" and "liberal"
retain their usefulness, today's liberal-minded Protestant reveals an orthodoxy that would have surprised his
nineteenth century namesake.

Both in theology and in preaching, as well as in the life
of the Church in general, there exists more interest in the
supra-individual, transcendent and normative dogma.
Undoubtedly, the influence of the great theologian Karl
Barth has contributed to that, for his theology is sometimes referred to as a "Copernican revolution." During a
long period, Reformational theology, at least in
German-speaking lands, seemed to be centered on man's
religious sentiment as its fulcrum. Now, however, this
theology more and more begins to realize that the measure
of all things is not man but God and His Word. Formerly
the Bible was made far too innocuous by "enlightened"
trainers; and erudite scholars all too often reduced it to a
manifesto of a more or less rationalistic humanism. Now
the Bible can again address authoritative and normative

words to man, and it is respected even if it tells him things which he himself did not think of.

In his time Soren Kierkegaard had already complained that the anthropocentric interpretation of the Bible "interprets and interprets Christ's Word for so long a time that it gets its own meaning out of it, the prosaic (the trivial)—and now that it has removed all difficulties it is reassured and appeals to Christ's Word."[4] With all the literary means at his disposal Kierkegaard battled against the implicitly accepted general opinion that the Bible, somehow, ultimately says in a lofty way exactly the same as we ourselves could have said. The result of the accepted Bible interpretation in his days was that godliness was nothing but a frank-hearted enjoyment of life. Writing in his diary, Kierkegaard noted:

> Suppose that in the New Testament it were written, for example (a thing we can at least suppose), that every man shall have $100,000. . . . Do you believe that then there would be any question of a commentary? —or not rather that everyone would say: That is easy enough to understand, there is absolutely no need of a commentary, for God's sake, let us be delivered from any commentary. But what is actually written in the New Testament (about the narrow way, about dying to the world) is not a bit more difficult to understand than that about the $100,000. The difficulty lies elsewhere, in the fact that it is not to our liking—and therefore, therefore, therefore we must have commentaries and professors and commentaries. It is to get rid of doing God's will that we have invented learning . . . ; we shield ourselves behind tomes.[5]

Kierkegaard's diatribes against the Scriptural sciences were one-sided and applicable only to his time. Bible

---

4. *The Instant*, XIV, 235.
5. Quoted in W. Lowrie, *Kierkegaard*, Vol. 2, New York, 1962, p. 539.

exegetes have done their part in freeing the Scriptures
from the straitjacket of the Enlightenment, just as they
had first contributed to disarming the Bible. The books of
Holy Writ need explanation and commentary; exegesis is
never superfluous. Nevertheless, it is true that the reading of the Bible presupposes in both the scholar and the
ordinary believer a certain willingness to listen and an
openness also from the standpoint of one's world view. In
many circles the nineteenth and early twentieth century
philosophy of life left hardly any room for such openness,
so that a long time had to pass before Kierkegaard's cry
was heard. It was only when Karl Barth sounded the
alarm that there was any question of a large scale awakening. Broad circles of the Reformational world marked
by an introverted theology that had degenerated into an
anthropocentric doctrine were converted by him to a reverend attention to God's transcendence and to His Message addressed to man but, nonetheless, transcending
man. Barth's theology is the theology of God's sovereignty.

Now the Bible is able again to offer man perspectives
that were formerly impossible. Such unexpected words
as: "Whoever leaves his father and his mother for My
sake and that of the Gospel" now again have a fair chance
of being heard. At the same time, however, it will still
remain true for all of us that we will have more difficulty
with passages of the Bible that we understand than with
others that are not clear to us (Mark Twain).

Separate mention must be made of another factor
within Reformational thought and life although this factor is connected with the above-mentioned interpretation
of the Bible. During the past decades there has arisen a
new attention to the idea of the Church, of the Body of
Christ. In the nineteenth century there often was an
enthusiastic piety centered on Christ, both in German

pietistic milieus and in French-speaking Calvinistic Christendom (Alexandre Vinet and Alphonse Monod), as well as in the various revival movements. But there was hardly any genuine ecclesial or community consciousness. Man's bond with God through faith was largely a question of an intense but individualistic relationship with Christ. Religion was a strictly personal affair. The idea that the apex of Christ's life, His resurrection, meant also the inauguration of a deeper bond among men "in Christ" did not play any role in prayer and the confession of one's faith.

On the larger scale of the Churches, too, there existed at that time a pious individualism. The various national Churches and the different denominations had little or nothing at all to do with one another. They did not feel any need for universalism or intercommunication and even less, of course, for intercommunion.

Yet there existed a Christian social awareness. The self-sacrificing love of Christ and His Sermon on the Mount undoubtedly were for many the basis of their missionary and charitable work. Nevertheless, the last article of the Creed, "I believe in one, holy, universal and apostolic Church," did not function existentially within their confession of the faith.

At present, however, ecclesial or communal consciousness stands more clearly in the foreground. The history of the Protestant ecumenical movement clearly shows the development of that consciousness. Significantly, it was the missions that constituted the cradle of this awakening Church consciousness. When they faced the practical issue of either interdenominational competition or Christian universalism, the missionary societies began to realize that faith in Christ was not merely a matter of personally responding to His call but, at the same time, of an entering into the community of Christ's Body. To become a Christian means to tear down dividing walls, to enter into communion, to object as a matter of principle to separation, seclusion and aloofness. The many efforts to arrive at practical collaboration were unwittingly borne by the reality of Christ's Body.

As this ecumenical consciousness spread from the missions to the Reformational Churches at large, the ecclesial meaning of being a Christian also expressed itself there more forcefully. Not only Life and Work were seen as objects of the ecumenical tendencies, but also Faith and Order. The visible Church is not an organization created by the faithful for practical purposes but a reality intended and willed by Christ. In their work, but also in their worship and expression of faith, men must begin to constitute, according to God's will, a single humanity, a single Body animated by God's power.

This Church consciousness influences the entire Christian view of life. The final stage of human history, for the realization of which God has engaged man's own endeavors, is no longer seen as a catastrophe accompanied by a possibility of survival and the hope of individual immortality. On the contrary, the end of all things is rather the glorious completion of the community, the finishing touch God gives to His creation. History, which is a history of salvation, ends in the realization of the apocalyptic vision: the final event is presented as a crisis giving birth to a new Jerusalem, a city with streets, a community, in full harmony with the New Man, although His Body continues to show the scars of the blows delivered by the old community—scars which now appear as signs of victory.[6]

Reflecting on this radical shift in Christian self-understanding, one can find everywhere traces of this

6. Cf. George F. MacLeod, *Only One Way Left. Church Prospect*, Iona Community, Glascow, 1956.

growing ecclesial or communal consciousness. The liturgy is wholly in motion. Aversion to the new and unfamiliar, which used to characterize this expression of religiousness, is now much less strong than formerly. People are less and less inclined to accept the liturgical *status quo*. They experiment with forms of worship that hitherto were the exclusive property of other denominations.

The growing consciousness that worship is a community affair is even more evident than the new flexibility of rubrics and forms of worship. The entire community is asked to participate in an active way. The eucharistic supper is increasingly interpreted in a more communal, even an interdenominational, manner. We may even say that the entire sacramental life meets with an increasing interest among practicing Protestants. In many places the question concerning sacramental confession, confirmation and the anointing of the sick now is raised in an unprejudiced fashion, while formerly such ideas belonged exclusively to the realm of polemical writings. Briefly put, for many Reformational Christians it is now a conviction of faith that the relationship between God and man has a visible social aspect, which is dominated by Christ and which, in accordance with God's will, also expresses itself liturgically in sacramental life.

At first sight one might feel inclined to consider this increasing ecclesial consciousness a victory for the clerical position. The reason is not only that we unwittingly continue to identify the Church with the clergy, but also that the liturgical renewal seems to refer merely to ritual matters. In the eyes of many, liturgical progress can wholly disregard "profane" life, just as the "world" can consider itself uninterested and dismiss the liturgical renewal with a shrug. However, this renewal has also definitely revitalized the awareness of not being concerned merely with ceremonial matters but with the believer's existential bond of service to his fellow-men as well. Church service has an unbreakable bond with the service of man's fellowmen.

The liturgy would be completely misunderstood if one were to conceive it as totally encompassed by a lofty play of ceremonies and rites performed with one's back turned to the world of daily life. Worship is not an aesthetic flight from the world. It is connected not only with the sanctuary but also with the city, as the Anglican Bishop John A. Robinson has argued so forcefully.[7] His plea for a clear, visible and liveable connection between daily life and Church worship is not just another attack of a secularizing Christianity on a sacred and inviolable heritage. It is not a plea against but for an authentic liturgy. The place where we stand is always sacred ground.

"Christ did not die in a cathedral between two burning candles." These words of George MacLeod, founder of the Iona Community, could easily be viewed as cheap criticism if it were not for the fact that he himself has made important contributions to the thoughtful development of a renewed liturgy. His words express an aversion to making the divine cult a pious play and amusement; they are not a rejection of the liturgy. When in a genuinely Christian way, that is, in a social and communal way, Christians have practiced living the new life with respect to one another and with respect to non-Christian fellowmen, when they have practiced reconciliation instead of blame, mutual care instead of conflict, then it is really time for them to go to church; there an essentially corporate Act is performed, in which we again and explicitly place our-

7. In a lecture delivered in 1958 at the Episcopal Theological Seminary of Alexandria, Va. Cf. his work, *On Being the Church in the World*, 2nd impr., London, 1961.

selves under the influence of the One who alone can create the New Community, the Body of Christ.[8]

When the liturgy is again understood as both worship and service of our fellow-men, we will also understand much better that "liturgy" and *"apartheid"* (separatism) do not march together. Perhaps our period in the history of salvation is destined to discover—or rather rediscover—that becoming a Christian is becoming a community man.

Viewed against this background, the revival of religious community life in the world of the Reformation becomes meaningful and can be understood.

8. Cf. George MacLeod, *We Shall Rebuild. The Work of the Iona Community on Mainland and on Island*, 2nd ed., Glascow, 1962, p. 81. It is to be noted that in the Bible the term "liturgy" has a much broader sense than we are accustomed to attribute to it. It extends to liberal assistance to fellowmen in need (2 Cor. 9:12), life itself, with all its difficulties, lived in a spirit of faith (Phil. 2:17), and simply being of service (Phil. 2:30).

CHAPTER TWO

THE COMMUNITY OF TAIZÉ

WE WILL HERE RECOUNT the history of one of the most famous Reformational religious groups, the Community of Taizé. All kinds of illustrated magazines, newspapers and religious monthlies have drawn attention to this community and provided the Brothers with a publicity which they undoubtedly look upon with mixed feelings. Part of that general interest is of course due to ordinary human curiosity, which is tickled by the mere fact that here are Protestants dressed in a monastic garb. Nevertheless, even this ordinary tourist curiosity may occasionally give rise to an encounter with the deeper reality underlying the Taizé phenomenon. For the relationship between occasion and effect in the domain of spiritual experience is obscure and unpredictable. "The publicity surrounding our community is a serious problem, of course," admitted the Prior of Taizé, but we are people of the twentieth century. We could not act as if we belonged to another century."[1] In the light of their ecumenical vocation the Brothers consider themselves obliged to be open to the endless stream of visitors to Taizé. The same principle induces them to put up with world-wide publicity. The phenomenon of Taizé belongs

1. Interview of the Prior with Michael van der Plas, *Elzeviers Weekblad,* September 22, 1962, p. 9.

to God and to the entire Church community at large; hence it is up to Him who called forth this phenomenon to decide if and how He wishes to make use of it.

If we wish to recount Taizé's history here, it is for the purpose of reflecting, together with the Brothers of Taizé, on the meaning and function of actual and possible community life within the Church and the world. This purpose justifies the theological considerations that preceded and that will follow this story. Frequently, however, the acts and especially the decisions of others are more eloquent than spoken or unspoken reflections. People who remain untouched, for example, by a theoretical dissertation about "possessing things in common" will sit up and take notice when they hear the story of certain deeds. An original initiative or activity is better than a new theory or a new terminology to enlighten people. Man may then suddenly realize how much he has resigned himself to the *status quo* and how many opportunities he has left unused.

The premises leading to the Community of Taizé must be sought in Lausanne in the year 1939, where its founder Roger Schutz, then twenty-four years old, attended the local university as a student in theology. He had then assumed the leadership of the *Féderation chrétienne des Etudiants,* and as such he attended its discussion groups. In the discussions of the students a constantly recurring factor was how much "uninvolvement" and individualism hampered one's being a Christian. Many a devout Christian, they felt, tries to live a Christian life alone and to face his spiritual problems in unaided solitariness. Unwittingly, perhaps, many of these students had separated their being-a-Christian from their professional contribution to society, as if the former belonged to their strictly private sphere and had nothing to do with their future leadership in the world. Their common Bible readings and common days of recollection clearly revealed how untenable such a view was. By way of these discussions and through common prayer and reflection, Roger Schutz gradually conceived a desire for an orderly spiritual and community life. This desire must have influenced also his choice of the topic for his licenciate dissertation, *The Monastic Ideal Until Saint Benedict and Its Conformity with the Gospel.*

For further reflection on his destiny he had also made retreats in Catholic monasteries, with the Carthusians of *La Grande Chartreuse* and with the Trappists. His time, however, was not entirely taken up with recollection and study. The misery caused in France by the war moved him and he felt called to do something about it. In the summer of 1940 he visited Burgundy to look for a starting point for his plans. A "notary" in Cluny referred him to a large empty house in a nearly abandoned village, Taizé, about six miles away. It had been built in the style of Louis XIII and used to belong to the Counts of Brie. A chance meeting in Taizé made Schutz decide to establish himself in that house. The date was August 20, 1940.

The first beginnings must have been far from easy. The village had then less than eighty inhabitants. Most of its former population had long ago abandoned it for industrial centers in the neighborhood, and a stubborn disease in the vineyards had done the rest. The few remaining villagers lived a withdrawn life and were full of suspicion against the intruders.

Taizé was close to the demarcation line between the "free" zone of France and the German-occupied part. Shelterless refugees, especially Jews but also members of the *Résistance,* found a welcome in Schutz' house. With a few of these people he began to make the most urgent repairs to the building and to clear the grounds of weeds.

Three times a day, however, he took time out to pray alone.

"From the start, I told myself that I could not claim to have achieved anything so long as my vocation as a Christian did not find an echo in the part of the world around me."[2] He sought contact with the people in his immediate surroundings who, according to the information he then had, were supposed to be Catholics. The ecumenical climate of those days, however, was still far from what it is today. Significantly, the Prior calls that period a "cold winter." Nevertheless, there were already some signs heralding the coming of spring. One of these was the *Abbé* Paul Couturier.

This priest lived in Lyons and had devoted his entire work to Christian unity and reunion. Toward Christmas 1940 Schutz went to pay him a visit. This was the beginning of a series of personal and written contacts which exercised an incalculable influence upon the future development of Taizé. Schutz at once recognized in Father Couturier a fellow Christian without deceit. He invited the priest to visit Taizé and offer Holy Mass there in the neglected twelfth century church. He himself would be present and take part in it to the extent that a Protestant could. In this way he hoped to enter into communication with the unfriendly and aloof villagers. As he wrote to Couturier on April 6, 1941, "It is really painful to live in the midst of the 'people of believers' and to remain nonetheless isolated." On June 9 he added: "Soon I will have the pleasure of seeing you here and, through you, enter into communion with the whole Church."

The little romanesque church, situated in the center of the village on top of the local hill, was in a sad state of disrepair and hardly ever used. The bell sounded only for

2. *Fêtes et Saisons*, Janvier, 1965, p. 11.

funerals. But on July 5 Roger Schutz hopefully pulled its rope. Father Couturier offered Holy Mass but, aside from Schutz and Maurice Villain (who had come with the priest), only a single old woman attended the service. This religious indifference of his immediate surroundings sometimes caused Schutz to wonder whether it would not be better to go elsewhere. But in the end he decided to stay.[3]

Schutz also used his contact with Couturier to ask the latter's advice about his planned daily rule. In the fall of the same year he composed a brochure of eighteen pages, entitled *La Communauté de Cluny. Notes explicatives.* We find there one of its central ideas expressed in three words which are still key words of the present rule: *Joy, Simplicity, Mercy.*

In September, 1942, Brother Schutz and Father Couturier met again, this time in the Trappist abbey of Les Dombes. Schutz was no longer alone, for two young men had joined him: Max Thurian, a theology student of Geneva, and Pierre Souvairan, a graduate of Zürich's polytechnical school who had specialized in agriculture. These three together were the first to lead a religiously inspired community life within the Calvinist tradition. While Schutz and Thurian were on a visit in Geneva at the end of 1942, the Swiss-German frontier was closed. The freedom of the unoccupied zone of France had come to an end, and Pierre Souvairan remained alone in Taizé. The forced stay of the other two in Switzerland, however, was not fruitless; for Schutz was able to present in 1943 his licenciate dissertation. He experienced some difficulties with the examination committee, which was not too eager to accept the thesis contained in the title of the dissertation: *The Monastic Ideal Until Saint Benedict*

3. Cf. Maurice Villain, *L'Abbé Paul Couturier, apôtre de l'unité chrétienne,* 3rd ed., Paris, 1959, pp. 177 ff.

and Its Conformity with the Gospel. The topic was indeed still too novel at that time.

During this period Schutz also organized bi-monthly colloquies which, in a way, were a continuation of the former Lausanne discussions about being-a-Christian in society. The two Brothers also paid much attention to the celebration of the liturgy. With the approval of local ecclesiastical authorities, they were able to experiment, and in the services which they were permitted to hold in the Saint Peter's cathedral at Geneva, they made a liberal use also of non-Calvinistic liturgical traditions. Today all this is commonplace, for now Protestants do not shy away from anything Catholic nor do Catholics any longer hesitate to sing certain traditionally Protestant hymns. But at that time the "cold winter" still reigned supreme, and the ecumenical spring had not yet started.

During these war years, community life also began to assume a more fixed form, and the group gained a new member in the person of another young man, Daniel de Montmollin. In 1945, when the frontiers were open again, the young community definitely established itself at Taizé, even though the villagers' aloofness had not changed. All kinds of rumors circulated among them. Such a strange community was bound to arouse suspicion, for the local people were unable to understand anything of the ideals animating these young men. The situation of the Brothers was indeed delicate: they were Protestants surrounded by people who were at least nominally Catholics. They would have liked to let their Christian inspiration radiate over their environment, but a sense of loyalty toward the Catholic Church forbade them to spread their ideals in the same way Catholic monks could have done it. Harassed by the evil tongues of the aloof villagers, Roger Schutz finally saw no other solution than to approach one of them in person and ask him to speak up and to state, in the name of Christ, what he had against the Community. This candid approach disarmed the opposition, and gradually the evangelical openness of the Brothers began to overcome the passive resistance of the local people.

One of Calvin's objections to religious communities had been that their members abandoned the position which God's providence had given them in society. The monks, he said, break the unity of the Church by founding a twofold Christianity. "When Augustine makes brotherly love the chief and almost only rule [of religious life], are we to think that he praises a conspiracy by which a few men, bound together among themselves, are separated from the whole body of the church?"[4] And: "All those who enter into the monastic community break with the church. Do they not separate themselves from the lawful society of believers in adopting a peculiar ministry and a private administration of the sacraments? If this is not to break the communion of the church, what is? . . . What resemblance do they [present day monks] have to the ancient monks? Even though they dwelt apart from others, yet they had not a separate church; they partook of the sacraments with the others; they attended solemn assemblies; they were a part of the people. By creating a private altar for themselves, what else have present day monks done but broken the bond of unity? For they have both excommunicated themselves from the whole body of the church and despised the ordinary ministry by which the Lord willed to preserve peace and love among his people."[5]

Similar considerations led the Brothers of Taizé to foster and develop with special care their bond with the

4. *Institutes of Christian Religion,* IV, 13, 10; in the Westminster Press, 1960, edition of Calvin's works, Vol. XXI, pp. 1264 f.
5. *Ibid.,* IV, 13, 14; Vol. XXI, pp. 1268-69.

neighborhood. It was not merely a question of doing this "in spirit," however. Using the income of their work (by now other members had joined their community), they undertook to take care of twenty war orphans. These boys were lodged in the second large house of the village, the Manor, and entrusted to the ministrations of Geneviève Schutz, a sister of Brother Prior. Brother Alain, the agricultural specialist, managed to make himself one with and welcome among the surrounding population by erecting a cooperative dairy, the usefulness of which was experienced by an ever-widening circle of farmers. Brother Robert, a physician, practiced in the village and its surroundings.

In the summer of 1947 Schutz and Thurian visited the most important Anglican religious communities, such as the Cowley Fathers of Oxford, for the purpose of orientation. Writing to Father Couturier from England, Brother Schutz gave thanks to God for having preserved him and his brothers from sectarianism. The forced isolation, imposed on them by the aloofness of their nominally Catholic surroundings, could easily have induced them to withdraw into themselves and assume an unecumenical attitude. Fortunately, however, they had been able to preserve and purify their Christian openness.

Since the time of the French Revolution there had been no priest attached to the little church of Taizé. It stood there dirty and neglected in a church yard overgrown with weeds, a sad reminder of different times. The Brothers of Taizé now addressed a letter to the Bishop of Autun, under whose jurisdiction the village belonged. They offered to clean and restore the church and asked his permission to use it for their liturgical services. Bishop Lebrun thought it prudent to consult the papal Nuncio, Msgr. Roncalli, the future Pope John XXIII. On the latter's advice the bishop consented. On Easter Sunday,

1948, the five Brothers for the first time were able to use the little church for their common prayer of the office. The bishop's permission had stipulated that the church would remain diocesan property and that from time to time a priest would offer Holy Mass in it; on the other hand, the Brothers could use it for their office and their celebration of the Eucharist.

During all this time the Brothers continued to reflect upon the form their lives were to assume. It would be wrong to think that the first members had come to Burgundy with a pre-established and firm program laid down in writing which they intended now to put into practice. As they themselves declare, most of their ideas arose in a community way through discussion and common prayer. These ideas were then tested in a communal way, in which deliberation was supported and accompanied by actualizing prayer. It may be worthwhile to dwell somewhat longer on this point. For in our world of technology and the "organization man" it is always possible that the proper character of Christian deliberation about finding the next stage on life's road will disappear under the pressure of a businesslike approach that disregards God's guidance.

There may be a certain danger in trying to throw light on the way one community acts by referring to ideas that originated in another community. Taizé was not influenced by the Anglican communities. Nevertheless, we think that the fundamental principles expressed by Roger Lloyd, the Warden of the Companies of the Servants of Christ the King,[6] are the same as those which guide the Taizé Community in its communal discussion. Lloyd writes:

> Our human initiative and energy must at all points depend on, and be linked to God's own. . . . The first

6. *An Adventure in Discipleship,* London, 3rd impr., 1955.

action required of all Christian people who care for the growth of the Kingdom of God is really the fostering of an attitude of mind towards God. They must yield and wait. They must be filled with expectancy. . . . This attitude of mind which stakes all on the initiating energy of God is only fully fruitful when the mind which holds it is deliberately laid alongside other minds which are thinking in the same way. . . . Individual submission is only completed when it is made in company with others. . . .

God wants to guide us. He can only do so if we ask Him for it and wait in silence to receive it.[7]

In the publications of Taizé's theologians, one sometimes finds a warning that the book in question "does not theologically commit the Community of Taizé." While such a warning undoubtedly is not meaningless, it does not imply that the ideas to which the book bears witness grew and developed entirely without the community. There is every reason to assume that, especially with respect to positions that draw attention in controversial matters, they are the fruit of fraternal discussions, common prayer and a communal liturgical life.

It was also in this way that the first Brothers of Taizé constantly reflected in common discussion on the next step on their road. Everything developed in a groping fashion, not because the Brothers hesitated or wondered, but as a matter of principle. In subsequent years their Prior frequently drew attention to the organic, that is, gradual, way in which God gives guidance, using mutual consultation and the fullest possible information as His tools. A visiting tourist may view the matter as a kind of democracy, but in reality it is a question of dependence on God in togetherness. The divine purpose is the creation of mankind as a corporate body. Consequently, mankind shall give response to God as a people, and it shall do this together. For this reason there is such a thing as the

7. *Ibid.*, pp. 19 and 59.

Church. This ecclesial reality finds visible expression in authentic communities. Dependence upon the initiative of God, waiting upon Him, is to be combined with a right, free and equal use of human reason. For this reason the Brothers of Taizé travelled for orientation purposes to England, maintained contacts with Catholic priests and monasteries in the neighborhood, as well as with worker-priests, and studied tradition. But the first concern of the community was to yield to whatever form of life the Holy Spirit wished them to assume.

Roger Schutz has often been asked whether the Community of Taizé wanted to imitate traditional monastic life when they decided to put their possessions in common and live as celibates under authority. His answer was:

> We reasonably tried not to let ourselves be influenced by the experiences of the past. We wanted to begin with a clean slate, in order to live and experience everything afresh. Yet the day came when we realized that we could not stay in our vocation without obliging ourselves fully to putting our goods in common, submitting to an authority and celibacy.[8]

In this way the Taizé community gradually developed its spirituality and its rule. Slowly also the idea began to gain ground that God's faithfulness and man's confidence in God could assume the form of a definitive bond. On Easter Sunday, 1949, the first seven Brothers pronounced their "lifelong commitment." They had come from different countries and belonged to distinct and separate Churches. It was not indifferentism that had joined these men from different denominations into a single commu-

8. Schutz, "Die Entstehung von Kommunitäten in den Kirchen der Reformation," *Frei für Gott und die Menschen*, Stuttgart, 1959, p. 43.

nity of life. Their union did not mean that in their eyes
the differences did not matter. But they thought and had
discovered that the things that bound them together were
greater than those that separated them. In their community of life they gave a vivid expression to their belief in
the power of Christ to create unity and to form a Body.
The influence of the risen Lord, who came to end man's
dividedness and to bring about reconciliation, is stronger
than the sin of men's divisiveness and tendency to remain aloof from one another. Today, after so many years
of experience, Brother Schutz characterizes the Brothers'
togetherness as "unanimity in pluralism." "To live unanimity in pluralism is to seek the pivot common to all, the
pivot around which diversity is built in a pluralism of
expression, in a freedom of existence that is all the greater
according as the unanimity is more secure."[9] As Christians, the Brothers had precisely entrusted themselves to
this power of Christ and had been called to communion.
It is hardly necessary to point out that the diversity[10] of
denominations within a single community endows the
latter with a universal receptivity that is of particular
importance for ecumenical work.

Since that first profession in 1949, the number of
Brothers has continued to increase. Now there are nearly
seventy. Most of the Brothers come from the liberal
professions. This phenomenon also deserves attention.
Beyond doubt, it is a blessing for Taizé that it is not a
clerical community dominated by theologians or men
whose principal function is pastoral care. The Brothers'

9. Schutz, *L'Unanimité dans le pluralisme*, Taizé, 1966, p. 7.
This book is hereafter quoted as *L'Unanimitĕ*.
10. The doctrinal unity existing in the Churches of the Reformation makes it possible for the Brothers to live in community
and to be in communion with one another, while retaining their
ecclesiastical allegiance. We will return to this matter in Parts
Three and Four.

professions cause them to mix daily with people from all
kinds of milieus and having different interests. Their
clothing does not distinguish them in any way from their
colleagues outside the community. The only distinguishing mark by which a careful observer could recognize
them as Brothers is a silver ring, the sign of their religious commitment or profession. One of the Brothers is a
physician. For many years he took care of a regular medi-
cal practice in the village. He had his regular office hours
and also visited patients at their homes. His work greatly
contributed to making the young community accepted in
the village and its environment. Another Brother is an
architect; still others run the printshop, paint, or produce
ceramics and art work in wrought metals, wood and en-
amel. Within the community, work is divided in such a
way that a maximum balance is guaranteed. Several
Brothers who had pursued higher studies before their
entrance have since then also learned a useful or fine art;
others study or have added a complementary intellectual
orientation to their former training.

Aside from the diversity of professions which makes it
possible to maintain contact with widely divergent milieus, there is another factor that needs to be mentioned,
viz., the dispersion of the community's building throughout Taizé. The traditional picture which the term "monastery" evokes among Catholics is a kind of spiritual for-
tress with a well-rounded enclosure. Whatever osmosis
there is with the world takes place by way of a Brother
Porter and parlor rooms. In other words, there is a "bottle-
neck" effect: the broad stream of the world must be
pressed into a channel if it is to enter through the narrow
gate. Taizé also has its closure, of course, for the endless
stream of visitors would impede the functioning of the
community if anyone could freely enter anywhere in
their house. Not all Brothers live in the Community

house, however; several of them dwell in lodgings that "psychologically" belong to the village complex of structures. In many respects the Brothers are "fellow townsmen" of the "ordinary" people. This fact makes it so much easier for them to fulfill their task of representing the Church as community than it is for the traditional Catholic monasteries of priests or "clericalized" congregations of Brothers.

In an article that speaks in a very general way about communities within the world of the Reformation, Roger Schutz draws attention to this "lay aspect":

> Just as the religious community is a sign for the Church, so also must it be a sign *in the world*. In a certain respect this community is a lay community. Even if within its own bosom it needs an ecclesiastical or clerical office to take care of preaching, the administration of the sacraments, spiritual guidance and the connection with the Church, all members nonetheless must consider themselves laymen in the Church. They must remain very close to the modern world, through their work which offers them a living, through an existence that does not separate them from their fellowmen.[11]

Speaking in particular about Taizé, the Prior says:

> The Reformation tries to develop a positive element by forming a current of openness to the world. We find the same kind of attention to being open to the world at the beginning of religious community life. Neither Saint Basil nor Saint Benedict wanted to establish clergy societies in the early centuries of the Church. So far as we ourselves are concerned, we, too, have tried to connect action and contemplation.[12]

11. Schutz, *Frei für Gott und die Menschen,* p. 40.
12. *Ibid.,* p. 42.

Only ten per cent of the Brothers are ministers and have as such gone through a complete theological education. All of them, however, had been ministers before joining the Community. In Taizé itself no one has ever been ordained for the ministry or even orientated in that direction after entering. Yet, this is merely a *de facto* existing situation and not a matter of principle.

The probationary period or novitiate also has gradually assumed a more fixed form. It lasts about three years. The three pillars of spiritual formation offered during the novitiate are study of the Bible, Church history and sociology. The Bible is studied because Scripture contains the fundamental inspiration for their religious and liturgical life. Church history is offered because this study can open the mind to the distinction between what is permanent and inviolable both on the part of man and on the part of the Gospel and, on the other hand, the various forms in which these permanent dimensions find expression. The sensitivity for the distinction between the absolute and the relative that is developed in this way is bound to exercise a beneficial influence on the best possible ecumenical attitude. It prevents one from swearing too easily by the old and the familiar. Thus, this formation in Church history lays the basis for ecumenical adaptability. Sociology, finally, serves to give the Brothers a clear and objective awareness of the situation in the world: its analphabetism, hunger, its problems of armament and overpopulation;[13] an awareness also of the non-theological factors involved in the divided condition of Christianity. In this way this study lays the foundation for a concrete solidarity with one's fellow-men.

In 1952 Taizé sent its first Brothers out "on missionary

13. In an interview about Taizé Prior Schutz said: "The figures [of statistics] are signs made by God" (Les chiffres sont les signes de Dieu), *La France catholique*, Jan. 13, 1961.

work." The plan for this mission had been developed through contact with worker-priests. The Brothers went to work in industrial plants at Monceau-les-Mines and later as construction workers in Marseille. They lived in rented apartments, two or three together and tried to follow as much as possible the daily rule of Taizé, including the office in common. The idea of "sharing the fate of their fellow-men" assumes a very clear form in these little "fraternities." They are established, but without any permanent character, at locations that enable the Brothers occupying them to act as advanced posts or "tendrils" of social or ecumenical importance. For instance, a few Brothers went to live in the Mohammedan country of Algeria, so severely tried in the political and economic realms. In a region where people are at least nominally in agreement about the Gospel there is a possibility that certain aspects of the Gospel which tend to remain hidden can be existentially rediscovered in their original sense in such a "diaspora" situation. It is the experience of these "fraternities" that keeps alive and nourishes the social feeling of involvement which sparks Taizé's concern about the lopsided division of earthly goods and the duty which the prosperous Christian world has with respect to the misery of the non-Christian world. Other Brothers worked in Abidjan on Africa's Ivory Coast, in the industries of Sheffield, and also in Coventry. In places like Coventry, with its many divided Christian denominations, the "fraternity" functioned as a kind of ecumenically sensitive cell of the Taizé community. Invited by the Coventry Cathedral, the Brothers also took part in the ministry. Two of them were the first wardens of the Cathedral's Chapel of Unity.

At least once a year all Brothers on mission return to Taizé to exchange experiences, gather new strength and discuss whether a particular "fraternity" should be continued or discontinued. In 1959 Prior Schutz told me that, insofar as it is possible, those Brothers who habitually reside in Taizé also undertake to live for some time in one of the "fraternities" as a kind of second novitiate. For the danger is not at all imaginary that otherwise they would install themselves in the closed community of like-minded people as a kind of ghetto and forget the need of the Church and of the world at large or consider such concerns merely from an ivory tower as an academic point of view. "In the world" the proper character and concreteness of the Gospel meet with new opportunities. The Brothers live in those vanguard "fraternities" for periods varying from three months to two or three years.

To conclude this enumeration of activities, we may make special mention of one particular form of presence and involvement. In 1958 Pope John XXIII, at the request of Cardinal Gerlier, had consented to receive Prior Schutz and Max Thurian in a private audience "on condition that they do not ask me questions that are too difficult." This encounter took place two days after the Pope's coronation. It was the first of a series of contacts with this pope whose actions, as the Brothers said, "have profoundly marked our lives." They resulted in the Pope's personal invitation to the Community of Taizé to send two of its members to the Council as observers. During all of the Council's sessions there was a "fraternity" at Rome, consisting of the Prior with his fellow-observer and three or four other Brothers to safeguard as much as possible common prayer and community life. Together the Brothers exercised a "ministry of welcome and presence." They often shared their meals with participants in the Council, bishops, observers, theologians and lay auditors. During the fourth session alone nearly five hundred came to lunch or dine with them. Writing to his confreres in Taizé, the Prior said:

Regarding ourselves, the signs of friendship we receive have been very impressive. This means that much is demanded of those who bear the name of Taizé, for the stock of confidence in us has never been so great. We are often consulted and much is expected of us. This credit must make us very attentive to the answers we give; they must proceed from reflection nourished at the springs of a contemplative life. Often it is silence that suffices, rather than giving answers at any cost. And even more is expected from the sign constituted by our very existence.[14]

In 1952–53 Roger Schutz edited *The Rule of Taizé*, of which a more detailed commentary appeared in 1960 under the title *Vivre l'Aujourd'hui de Dieu*.[15] The same year saw the publication of the Office of Taizé,[16] which enjoyed an immediate and great success both in France and abroad. It gave inspiration to the reorganization of morning and night prayers in Catholic religious communities and seminaries.

More important than these miscellaneous items of information, however, is to reflect, together with the Brothers, on the inner motives and driving forces that should animate an authentic Christian community life. The following chapters will attempt to record such reflections.

14. *Aujourd'hui, Journal de Taizé*, no. 13, Jan., 1966, p. 1.
15. *The Rule of Taizé*, French and English text, Packard Manse, Stoughton, Mass., 1961. *Living Today for God*, Helicon, 1962.
16. *Office de Taizé*, 3rd ed., Les Presses de Taizé, 1964.

PART TWO

THE VOCATION TO
RELIGIOUS COMMUNITY
LIFE AND THE
FUNDAMENTAL RULES:
COMMUNITY OF GOODS,
CELIBACY, ACCEPTANCE
OF AUTHORITY

To help us to remain faithful in this service of God there have been given us three great signs which constantly recall to us the absolute character of our vocation. ROGER SCHUTZ[1]

1. *Living Today for God*, p. 92.

CHAPTER THREE

GOD'S CALL AND MAN'S RESPONSE

1. Listening to the Call

> *A vocation is revealed by the light of the Holy Spirit*
> *which creates peace and joy; by a man's past life and*
> *present circumstances interpreted as signs of God's*
> *providence; in the act of faith and the self-commitment*
> *based on the Word of God; and by the counsel of the*
> *Church.* MAX THURIAN[1]

IN HIS BOOK *Marriage and Celibacy* Max
Thurian has tried to systematize the signs by which, in
general, God's call to celibacy is revealed in human life.
The New Testament, as we know, attempts to catalog
and name the effects of the Holy Spirit's active presence
in human existence on the basis of the experience of
Christian life. Similarly, on the basis of what that guiding impulse effects in consciousness, Brother Thurian
tries to describe the impulse of the Holy Spirit that leads
someone to the practice of Christian celibacy. Just as in
the case of St. Paul, so here also the "fruits" of the Holy
Spirit, however much they are gifts, are nevertheless
also active human attitudes of minds and choices of men.
That which is brought about by the Holy Spirit is ac-
tively, not passively, received. To be moved by the Spirit

1. *Marriage and Celibacy,* London, 1959, p. 88.

of God means that we ourselves go, choose and decide.

It seems to me that, with the necessary adaptations, we can also make use of the criteria established by Max Thurian with respect to the gift and vocation of celibacy, for the recognition of a vocation to religious community life in general.

According to Thurian, this gift is first of all an "interior witness of the Holy Spirit; this produces joy and peace in the consideration of this vocation rather than another."[2] Here also, as in faith, the decision is finally made by a value judgment, not by a rational criterion. In regard to celibacy Thurian remarks that it is always a part of a more general vocation. For instance, we begin to realize that we are called to a special and difficult apostolate and that this apostolate is possible only if we renounce family life because of the great demands it will make on our person or for other reasons; or we realize that we are called to the contemplative life, which demands great spiritual freedom; or we gradually understand that we are called to community life, to an availability in togetherness for some service or witness in the Church.[3]

This growing understanding and insight we acquire by means of the signs which are the divinely controlled but which are seemingly capricious circumstances of life's historical developments.[4] No awareness of a vocation is possible outside the context of a true faith in Providence. It is necessary to believe that our life is not a concatenation of accidental and bizarre events, but the unfolding and realization of a plan, conceived and actualized by the sovereign Lord who accompanies us in our lives; without such a conviction, there is no notion or awareness of an actual vocation and therefore also no question of an obe-

2. *Op. cit.*, p. 86.
3. *Ibid.*
4. *Ibid.*

dient discovery of a vocation. It is possible to speak of a "vocation" in the restricted sense of the term only if we admit that the whole of life includes an expectation of God and that every situation contains a new call of God.

Faith in an active presence of God lies at the basis of a vocation with respect to both its discovery and its fulfillment. In order to be able to live in and be animated by our vocation, it is necessary for us to have faith in the fact that, above all the forces at work in our lives, God's influence is the most decisive, the most truly determining factor. If this faith in God's providence disappears, then the faith in a particular vocation also vanishes.

If awareness of a vocation is part of a true act of faith in God's guiding providence throughout life, then evidently great stress must be placed on the fact that following the call to religious community life is an act of faith, a decision of faith.[5] No one ever has a metaphysical or mathematical certitude regarding the authentic foundation of his choice. Like any decision based on faith, following a vocation is a leap in the dark. Sometimes a vocation becomes more evident and more certain only after the decision and commitment have been made. It is God's will that the just live by faith; that is to say, one must often make more or less blind decisions in which a trusting self-surrender prevails over a detailed survey of life. Only on rare occasions does God indicate by means of logical reasonings, objective criteria and miraculous signs what man must do. We should be grateful to Him when He grants such "indubitable" certainties, but they are not necessary to enable us to answer and follow God's call.

Of course, all this does not mean that following a vocation is characterized by arbitrariness, that it is a gamble

5. Thurian, *op. cit.*, p. 87.

or taking a chance. The decision is made in a process of reconnoitering, with the eyes of faith, one's life situation and the call contained in it, one's aptitude for community life, and in allowing oneself to be enlightened by God's guiding Word through faithful reading of the sacred Scriptures.

Moreover, the Christian is never alone when he makes decisions of faith and endeavors to recognize God's will in a particular situation. He is assisted by the Church, by the community in which he lives, and by counsels that help him in discerning his vocation. In this way he avoids the subjectivism that constantly threatens to make his choice too personal.[6] The advice of his brethren in the faith, especially faith in God's providence, will give to his choice and commitment an objective character that acts as a powerful support in moments of doubt. Even more powerful is the support of the Church's presence when this support finds expression in a liturgical confirmation of his religious commitment or profession.

In this way, the Christian with the help of the community, can find assurance against paralyzing doubts that stifle activity and make decisions impossible; and the certainty of one's vocation can be endowed with the maximum of objectivity that is possible in this matter. The Christian receives such a firmness not only in the liturgical profession in a religious community, which acts as a confirmation of a matured certainty; but in an analogous way we may say the same with respect to the religious bond of marriage and the imposing of hands in conferring an ecclesial office.[7]

2. A Perpetual Commitment

The moment we make a covenant with Christ, He joins Himself to us. ROGER SCHUTZ[8]

6. *Ibid.*
7. Thurian, *op. cit.*, p. 99.
8. *Living Today for God*, p. 100.

In 1944 Prior Schutz wrote that the conditions established by the members for their community life; *viz.*, community of goods and celibacy, were not at all "perpetual vows."[9] For, promises made for life chain, as it were, the freedom of the Holy Spirit in human decisions implying that the Spirit could not make another call upon a man, outside the community structure, in the course of his life. Moreover, it seemed presumptuous on the part of any Christian to look at his life with a surveying glance and then to promise a particular way of life to God; for he would appear to lay claim to an unshakeable fidelity with respect to all of life's events, all its foreseen and unforeseen circumstances.

Nevertheless, on Easter Sunday, 1949, the first seven Brothers made their perpetual profession. Evidently, their attitude toward a life-long commitment had changed together with their understanding of the significance of such a commitment. Max Thurian explains the considerations that led to this change of view in the following way:

> The Brother who binds himself definitely to the Community henceforth establishes all his faith, all his expectations and all his joy *on the promise of Jesus Christ:* "Truly, I say to you, there is no one who has left house or brothers or sisters or mother or father or children or lands, for My sake and for the Gospel, who will not receive a hundredfold now in this time, houses and brothers and sisters and mothers and children and lands, with persecutions, and in the age to come eternal life" Mk. (10:30).
> Yes, the Brother knows and experiences every day that the *fruits* of this wonderful *promise* are not commensurate with his conviction of his vocation, with his faith and his powers. But he knows that Jesus Christ promises a hundredfold of all that was given up by

9. Schutz, *Introduction à la vie communautaire*, Paris, 1944, p. 29.

someone who in the obscurity of his faith took the decisive step in the community of his Brothers. And in moments of doubt and weariness, amidst those persecutions . . . which Christ in His infinite wisdom has foreseen, he relies solely on that *promise* made by God's Word, the Word that is found uniformly in the first three Gospels. . . .

The commitment does not make divine freedom powerless; on the contrary, in the order of vocation it makes the will of God more evident. If the commitment were only temporary, it would favor one's own will and subjectivism in the order of obedience to one's vocation, as well as an unsteadiness that is not to be underestimated regarding both community life and the Brother himself.

Only a commitment that is held to be unbreakable permits us to leave to God the responsibility for our vocation. . . . If the commitment is conceived in this way, it guarantees the necessary abdication of one's will and, at the same time, God's, freedom and sovereignty are also safeguarded; the objectivity of God's call is likewise preserved, for this call asserts itself, not through the conscience of the individual who is often cloistered within his own subjectivity, but through the more trustworthy channel of the praying community. This concept of the commitment assumes that truth has a better chance of manifesting itself in a community than through the individual, and that God's freedom and sovereignty are more clearly known when we renounce our own freedom and bind ourselves to Christ through a decision of obedience and love.[10]

Can man foresee all the circumstances of his life? Is it not more prudent to make decisions only for short periods of life, periods that one can grasp with a surveying glance? This question is concerned with the possibility for man to remain faithful, and it applies also to other decisions for life, such as that of marriage.

10. Max Thurian, "La Communauté de Cluny," *Verbum Caro,* vol. 2 (1948), pp. 115 f.

The same question can be asked on a more profound level. Is it possible for man to acquire a sufficient insight into his own true identity to make this insight serve for the orientation of his life? The human person is both a single unit and extended over history. Both of these poles must be taken into account when one attempts to answer our question. When he makes a decision for life, man takes up his own identity, and he does so in faith, taking this term in both its natural and its Christian sense.

The Brothers of Taizé like to emphasize God's sovereignty which finds expression in the perpetual profession. Man can dispose of his life only in dependence upon God. God's right of disposal is safeguarded against the individual's vacillating moods and subjective views. An individual's perpetual profession can, at the same time, promote his unity, integrity and identity.

When Catholics consider perpetual vows, there is a tendency to focus attention on the performance of *man*, on the risk and the venture, the prognosis concerning the sufficiency of one's own power. In other words, the *promise of man* stands in the center of interest. Members of the family wonder what the young man or woman is going to do; the candidate pronounces the formula of his promise to God amidst the oppressive silence of the gathering: "I make forever to God the vows of poverty, chastity and obedience." A fearful gift to God, one which makes a person think twice before he pronounces it. The ceremonial of the perpetual profession often accentuates the strain of the moment by introducing a few minutes of "earnest reflection" while the community chants the Litany of the Saints with its petitions to ward off all kinds of evil.

The Community of Taizé, however, centers the attention on *God's promise* to man. Its ceremony of profession stresses God's gift, expressed in a general way in the

Gospel, but now specifically directed to this man. It strikes a note of confidence, gratitude and joy. God commits Himself! On the day of profession an exhortation is read, not to warn the candidate for the last time that he should reflect on what he is about to do, but to make him realize what *God is doing:*

> Brother, you who commit yourself to God's mercy, remember that the Lord Christ comes to stengthen your feeble faith and that, in covenant with you, he fulfils for you the promise: Truly, there is no one who has given up home, brothers, sisters, mother, father, wife, children, land, for my sake and for the Gospel, who will not receive in this age a hundred times as much—houses, and brothers, and sisters, and mothers, and children, and land—and persecutions besides; and in the age to come eternal life. This is a way opposed to all human reason, but like Abraham, you can advance on this path only by faith, not by sight, always assured that he who loses his life for Christ's sake shall find it.[11]

The perpetual commitment is seen as an act of confidence in God. For this reason the Brothers of Taizé were somewhat hesitant to use the term *vows* and sometimes preferred the word *commitment. Vow* refers primarily to one's own achievement and also emphasizes more the various distinct obligations. *Commitment* points to the totality of life and to one's dedication. It better expresses the bond with Christ "in a dynamic forward movement."[12] However, the opposition of the two terms is not felt as an absolute. As a matter of fact, in the English edition of the rule, the three commitments are listed in the table of content under the title, "The Vows," while the text of the profession itself uses the title, "Commitments Made at the Profession."[13]

11. *The Rule of Taizé,* p. 70.
12. Schutz, "Die Entstehung von Kommunitäten in den Kirchen der Reformation," *Frei für Gott und die Menschen,* p. 44.
13. *The Rule of Taizé,* pp. 6 and 76.

The Brother finally and radically leaves the responsibility for his vocation to God: it is He who calls. He does not consider himself presumptuous when he confidently abandons himself to God and His promises, for there is no presumption in confessing that God is trustworthy.

The praying assembly of the community is an integral part of the perpetual profession. It is in this assembly that God's personal call receives a significance that goes beyond the merely subjective. It is also this community that certifies the validity of God's promise (Mk. 10:30) for this particular Brother and that, in God's name, officially applies the promise to him. Finally, "not only the relationship to God but also the solidarity with men, or brothers, are engaged by the 'I will' of the profession."[14]

Before reproducing here the ceremonial of the religious profession used in Taizé, we would like to draw attention to the fact that not only the content of the formulas but the entire liturgical procedure indicates the important role played by the community in this commitment. Those who are familiar with the religious profession ceremonies in many Catholic communities will undoubtedly be struck by the significant difference. The Catholic ceremony is also characterized by the dialogue of question and answer between the religious community, as represented by the superior, and the new member to be professed. But this dialogue does not go beyond a kind of legal precaution:

"Have you reflected sufficiently on the step you are about to take?"

"Do you persevere in your intention?"

"Do you realize that your commitment cannot be broken save by a special dispensation of the Holy See?"

Then the dialogue of the community and the new mem-

14. Schutz, *L'Unanimité*, p. 105.

ber is ended, and the community limits itself to the function of being a silent, legally required witness. The dialogue disappears entirely: Christ Himself is not addressed but watches only as a witness ("In the presence of Our Lord Jesus Christ"); similarly God Himself occurs only in the third person: "I make to God the three vows. . . ."

Thus, the profession is no longer a liturgical dialogue but the pronouncement of a declaration, listened-to by the community and by God. It is a solemn juridical procedure, a legally undisputable, irrevocable act drawn up with perfect clarity. The community's representative, on his part, concludes the ceremony with the contractual statement that the new member's declaration is legally binding and accepted as such by the community: "Henceforth you share in all the rights, favors and privileges of the professed members." The danger of a certain Pelagianism is not wholly imaginary, for throughout the entire ceremony there is a strong, almost exclusive emphasis on the "I" of the one who pronounces in a type of monologue the profession formula and on what he undertakes to do.

In the profession ceremonial of Taizé there are no invitation for renewed reflection and no final warnings, but an exhortation at the beginning indicates at once that which should stand at the center of attention; *viz.*, God's trustworthiness. God commits Himself, and the new member to be professed is reminded of this. Above we reproduced a part of this exhortation. When it is finished, the pronouncement of the profession follows in the form of this dialogue between the Prior as representing the community and the candidate:

Will you, through love of Christ, consecrate yourself with your whole being to Him?

I will.

Will you, henceforth, fulfil the service of God in our Community, in communion with your Brothers?

I will.

Will you, in renouncing all ownership to property, live with your Brothers not only in community of material goods, but also in the community of spiritual goods, while striving for openness of heart?

I will.

Will you, in order to be more available to serve with your Brothers and to give yourself completely to the love of Christ, remain celibate?

I will.

Will you, in order that we may be but one heart and one soul, and that our unity of service may be fully realized, assume the decisions made in Community and as expressed by the Prior?

I will.

Will you, while always discerning Christ in your Brothers, be watchful with them on good days as well as bad, in abundance as in poverty, in suffering as in joy?

I will.[15]

In this profession formula we have reached the three pillars of religious community life; *viz.*, the community of goods, celibacy and the acceptance of authority.

15. The profession is made during the Easter Vigil, after the renewal of the baptismal promises. Psalm 126 is sung with the antiphon: "He that goes forth weeping bearing the seed for sowing shall come home with shouts of joy." This is followed by a free prayer to the Holy Spirit, spoken by the Prior, a canticle to the Holy Spirit. Then the new Brothers are interrogated:

What do you ask?

The Mercy of God and the community of my brethren.

May God complete in you what He has begun.

Next, the Exhortation is made, and the Brothers pronounce their profession, which is signed on the Altar. After the kiss of peace they receive their rings with the words: "May this ring be the sign of our unity in the Lord"; then the hands are imposed on them and a stole is laid on them with the words: "Take upon you the yoke of the Lord, for his yoke is sweet and his burden light." A prayer closes this part of the Easter Vigil. The text of this liturgy may be found in *Liturgies pascales, Taizé*, 1962.

CHAPTER FOUR

COMMUNITY OF GOODS

If community of goods concerned only material goods, it would be very limiting; it should lead us to the community of spiritual goods, with its pains and its joys.
RULE OF TAIZÉ[1]

THE FIRST twelve chapters of the Acts of the Apostles want to make it clear that Christianity is possible only as community. This is an oft-forgotten truth. Through the reading of spiritual literature or the attendance of conferences in the past, many of us are familiar with the seductive but misguided view that the summit of the Christian ideal calls man to be "alone with the solitary God." The ideal of which the Acts speak is valid for all Christians: the company of those who believed in Christ were of one heart and one soul, and no one said that any of the things which he possessed was his own, but they had everything in common (Acts 4:32). God wills that the economic values constitute an inalienable part of the community which His creative love wishes to call forth on earth. The whole of life is the arena for the practice of Christianity and holiness. Thus when the religious group assumes the form of life marked by community of goods, this group's witness intends to empha-

1. *The Rule of Taizé and Spiritual Directives Following the Rule of Taizé,* p. 92.

size and make clearly visible a characteristic of Christian life that is valid for the entire Church.

The traditional term in Catholic circles for this commitment is "the vow of poverty." If we look at the formula of religious profession used at Taizé, we notice at once that this term is missing. True, the new Brother is asked whether he is willing to "be watchful with [his Brothers] on good days as well as bad, in abundance as in poverty, in suffering as in joy"—words which, let us mention it incidentally, strongly recall the traditional formula of the wedding ceremony: "for better for worse, for richer for poorer, in sickness and in health." What the Taizé Brother does promise is "community of goods" and, as the formula explicitly specifies, both spiritual (which includes intellectual and artistic) and material goods are included in this community. Let us begin here with a consideration of the community of spiritual goods.

1. Community of Spiritual Goods

When we hear about having goods in common, we are often inclined to think almost immediately and perhaps even exclusively of a community of material goods. Taizé points at once to a hierarchy of values: the community of goods finds its highest expression, not in the renunciation of one's possessions and their administration nor in the common use of things, but in the mutual and fraternal communication of spiritual goods. What is original or at least very striking in Taizé's considerations of the "community of goods" is the spiritual perspective opened by this commitment:

> Possessing goods in common takes on its true value only if it leads to a community of spiritual goods. Practicing frequent sharing of concerns with one another requires "transparency" of one man toward another.

This transparency does not imply pouring out confidences about oneself, but rather an openness of the whole person.[2]

This complete openness toward a fellow Brother is not easy. Such a community of spiritual goods requires a great measure of self-mastery.[3]

The community of goods concerns also the fruits of thought, as well as creative artistic work.[4]

As early as 1946 the Catholic ecumenical theologian Maurice Villain gave expression to the profound impression which this spirituality of mutual transparency had made upon him. Even then Prior Schutz already spoke about it "with a boldness and an originality . . . that deserve to be mentioned."[5] The Prior considers this "transparency" a necessary condition for the flourishing of the community. Every Brother should apply himself to that spirit of sharing, of simplicity, of nakedness of being.[6]

The community of goods in both the spiritual and the material sense must be particularly observed in the community meals. These brotherly encounters offer a special opportunity for mutual accessibility.

By way of their "community of spiritual goods" the Taizé Brothers discovered also the road to the confession of sins. For sin implies also an infraction of that spiritual belonging to one another. Sin is a taking back or keeping back of what one owes to the community. Hence if on the basis of God's forgiving grace a sinner recovers from his

2. Schutz, *Living Today for God,* p. 108.
3. Schutz, *Introduction à la vie communautaire,* Geneva, 1944.
4. *The Rule of Taizé and Spiritual Directives,* p. 92.
5. Villain, "La communauté protestante de Cluny," *Irenikon,* vol. 19 (1946), pp. 153-167.
6. Schutz, *Introduction* . . . , p. 46; Max Thurian, "La Communauté de Cluny," *Verbum Caro,* vol. 2 (1948), pp. 108 ff.

sin, this also implies that he recovers with respect to the community and that he is reinstated in full communion with it. This idea opens up a perspective on making a confession of his fault to a representative of the community and, on the part of the latter, a sign of forgiveness or absolution. At Taizé only Brothers who are ministers hear confessions. The *Spiritual Directives* of the Community contain an observation on this point:

> Man to man transparency does not mean to pour out one's heart, but limpidity of the whole person. Therefore, it would be a mistake to confuse openness to a Brother with confession; confession is done to the Lord of heaven and earth in the presence of a man who has received this ministry.[7]

These ideas are also present in the Catholic view of the sacrament of confession as an ecclesial reality. Community experience with confession undoubtedly constituted a great help for Max Thurian when he composed his work on confession.[8]

2. *Economic Witness of the Community of Goods*

The fact that Taizé places an original accent on the spiritual side of the community of goods does not mean that the Brothers are less interested in the problem of the Christian's relationship toward material goods. Till the present, and now perhaps even more than ever, the Community has always been occupied with the witness it must give with respect to the material world.

The preference given to the expression "community of goods" over the traditional "vow of poverty" fosters a wholesome honesty. As one of the Brothers told me, "We

---

7. *The Rule of Taizé and Spiritual Directives*, p. 132.
8. *La confession*, Paris, 1953; English edition, *Confession*, S.C.M. Press, London, 1959.

are sure of our daily bread; we cannot lay claim to the term 'poverty.'" Prior Schutz also writes: "Poverty is a term that burns the lips. In writing the Rule of Taizé, I hardly dared use it. It did not seem right."[8a]

"Blessed are you poor, for yours is the kingdom of God" (Luke 6:4). Voluntary poor could awaken somnolent Christians, they could perhaps liberate the Church from the "scandal of the evil rich" and contribute to the solution of the social question. "Poverty has no virtue in itself," warns the *Rule of Taizé*,[9] and the *Spiritual Directives* add: "One can live poorly and yet not radiate."[10] Poverty has religious significance to the extent that it means "to live without assurance of the morrow, in joyous confidence," to "live in the gladness of today."[11] In other words, poverty is meaningful insofar as it throws the Brothers and the community back upon God. As Prior Schutz writes in one of his works, "The spirit of poverty lies in the joy of the man whose security reposes on God and who, in consequence, is marked with external signs of gladness."[12]

The *Rule of Taizé* contains a warning against a puritanical view of the Gospel's "Blessed are the poor": "The spirit of poverty does not consist in pursuing misery, but in setting everything in the simple beauty of creation."[13] In the same line Prior Schutz argues: "If the spirit of poverty becomes synonymous with sadness and austerity, does it still really agree with the first beatitude?"[14] And in an interview with the correspondent of a French monthly he added: "The spirit of poverty is marked by signs such

8a. *Dynamique du provisoire*, Taizé, 1965, p. 69.
9. p. 53.
10. p. 89.
11. *Rule of Taizé*, p. 53.
12. *Dynamique du provisoire*, p. 70.
13. *Rule of Taizé*, p. 53.
14. *Dynamique du provisoire*, p. 70.

as joy, the colors of one's house—briefly, it has an exterior aspect that translates the simple beauty of creation."[15]

Especially since the Middle Ages the evangelical counsel of poverty has given rise to certain institutionalized forms which, as long as the world was not industrialized, held a genuine appeal. In that world riches meant primarily luxury and were of profit solely to the owner of wealth. Since the rise of industry, however, and the establishment of large enterprises the meaning of riches has undergone a drastic change. Gone is the primary implication of a life filled with excessive pleasures and of profits accruing solely to the owners' capital. Today ownership and capital are primarily a social-productive factor. Capital now means prosperity for many, the power to develop entire regions, to foster the growth of human society.

It stands to reason that this change implies also a modification of the meaning of evangelical poverty. A static clinging to its old significance, as if the world had not undergone any development, could conceivably change into its very opposite the entire power of witness that used to be attached to living the evangelical counsel of poverty. Clinging to the old meaning would be listening to the call of the Gospel in a form now rendered valueless. If poverty means not to possess any wealth or to abandon voluntarily one's wealth, then the significance of this poverty is quite different from what it used to be in the past. From a Christian and human standpoint it would be a serious omission to renounce "wealth" and, consequently, the opportunities to help certain segments of the world's population. Just as wealth is no longer a purely private affair but a social power of production, so

15. *Fêtes et Saisons,* Jan., 1965, p. 9.

also voluntary detachment from wealth is no longer only a matter of personal concern but possesses a social value or lack of value. To go begging instead of taking part in the work of developing the underprivileged can hardly hold today the same constructive meaning that it used to have in former times. The sacrifice that the Gospel demands of those who are moved by the Gospel's beatitude, "Blessed are the poor," is not to cease productive labor and to despise money as the "slime of the earth," but to develop to the fullest extent the opportunities which money, productive work, technical skill and equipment contain.

The Brothers of Taizé thought long and earnestly about the evangelical attitude a religious community should assume toward material goods. In the course of history material goods have often been a cause of division. Couldn't they acquire a unifying significance? Sharing in the world's misery is no longer a passive imitation of the poor's fate, but a participation in the struggle of the world against that misery. The Christian attitude toward material goods can take as its example Christ "who lived among sinners and understood their humanity. He changed water into wine at Cana to give them joy."[16]

Taizé acts on the principle that the Brothers themselves must provide for their own sustenance. "It has prevailed among us to refuse gifts for ourselves and to live by our work. So let us accomplish this work in all seriousness."[17] In Taizé itself the Brothers are busy in their printshop and ceramic works; others are painters, one is an agricultural expert, another is a physician; still others edit the periodical *Verbum Caro* or write books. In the various "fraternities" outside Taizé, some labor in local industry, in a hospital, or as clerks, truck drivers, longshoremen

16. Schutz, *Living Today for God*, p. 106.
17. Schutz, *L'Unanimité*, p. 41.

etc. This work allows some of their fellow-Brothers to devote themselves to unpaid functions, to study or to establish inter-church contacts and to gather ecumenical experiences.

"If community of goods were to lead us to abundance, our essential vocation would sooner or later, be impaired, without our being aware of it."[18] Religious community life contains the danger of a collective accumulation of possessions. The history of monastic life offered Prior Schutz abundant proof that such a development is never to the benefit of the community. As he declared in an interview with Sammy Chabrillan, "To live solely in a closed circle, to be willing only to provide for our own needs would be a serious mistake. If we do not think of giving, we will either work less or become rich."[19] And in a commentary on the Rule of Taizé, the Prior wrote recently: "Common life does not free us from preoccupation with daily bread, for we are asked not only to live by our work but also to sustain other people, in order to participate in a non-spiritualistic way in the *ecumene*, i.e., in the community of men throughout the world."[20] From the very beginning, therefore, the Brothers tried to prevent a socially useless accumulation of capital. They "invested" their surplus earnings in projects that were socially productive. For example, as we mentioned already, in its first years the Community took care of and provided food and lodgings for about twenty war orphans. In this context we can also recall the cooperative dairy organized by Brother Alain in 1954 and with which twelve hundred farms are now connected.

In 1961 Pope John XXIII recommended that the rural world organize itself in cooperatives. Taizé took this rec-

18. *The Rule of Taizé and Spiritual Directives*, pp. 87-88.
19. *Panorama chrétien*, no. 76, July, 1963, p. 21.
20. Schutz, *L'Unanimité*, pp. 42 f.

ommendation to heart. As Prior Schutz writes: "We then said to ourselves: 'We who have neither family nor anyone who expects his livelihood from us, let us use our freedom to bind ourselves on the agricultural level with those who are willing.'. . . We lay claim to the very principles of the first community of Jerusalem and we would like people to say of us: 'See how they love one another, they are of one heart and soul, they have everything in common.' And now, today, we have that community of goods with Christian laymen of a different denomination."[21] This new experiment is the COPEX, a radical cooperative venture, in which the Community of Taizé joined five farmer families of the neighborhood, young people trained by the French "Catholic Rural Action." The soil, cattle, agricultural tools and machines are now employed in common, while the profits are distributed, not on the basis of one's possessions, but on that of the work contributed to the enterprise. Since 1962 Taizé owns no land, cattle or agricultural implements, but is only a paid member of a collective enterprise. A legal contract valid for twenty years covers the COPEX, the "cooperative experiment."

COPEX can have many practical advantages, such as a greater specialization and a more rational distribution of labor, alternate free weekends, no more toil on the land by the farmers' wives and a more economic administration of business affairs. But the cooperative venture has also a more profound, a social and ecumenical meaning. With regard to the ecumenical aspect, Roger Schutz says:

> Together [with Christian laymen of a different denomination] we confront material reality, the question of money. It means that this summer we will have at our table some of these young farmers living in the neigh-

21. Interview published in *Fêtes et Saisons*, Jan., 1965, p. 11.

borhood. They will find a brotherly reception among us. And we, we will receive much in that dialogue with them, that exchange of views, that discussion of life between fathers of a family and ourselves, men consecrated to community life. . . . After living for two years in such close contact with young farmers, I am able to say today that we have discovered a new dimension of brotherly life and that there is no conflict between monastic life and, on the financial level, a demanding relationship with fathers of families.[22]

Once a thing has been done, it always seems to be much more the obvious thing to do than it really is. Let us recall that at first the Brothers experienced only aloofness at Taizé and that the five participating farmers are all convinced Catholics. If we try to transpose the experiment to a similar situation in our own surroundings, we are more likely to realize that something unusual has been accomplished at Taizé. Unusual as it is, however, tortuous arguments are hardly needed to bring it in contact with the Gospel.

"There was not a needy person among them," the Acts of the Apostles happily report; or rather, they offered this as an ideal of the Christian community, as the fulfilment of the Old Testament program: "There will be no poor among you" (Dt. 15:4). Accordingly, the community of goods is not conceived at Taizé in an "introverted" or centripetal way, but genuinely as an open and evangelical sharing of one's own. It is not a kind of consumers' league but solidarity, not a situation of enclave, but of insertion and collaboration. Undoubtedly we must view this as a revolution with respect to the traditional way monasteries are used to operate. It looks indeed very much like an evangelical dispossession to live in this way in a condition of habitual non-possession of goods. It is

22. *Ibid.*

very well possible that in the course of time "poverty" and the community of goods have become too much institutionalized in many Catholic monasteries and convents. Their economy is not open to inspection, and they often live in a temporal security that is not subject to the ups and downs of the economy which affects a large number of their fellow-Christians. We do not wish to say that many of these communities' activities do not require as a necessity a certain measure of economic stability. On the other hand, however, a more radical socialization of the material possessions belonging to religious communities, based on a more profound ecclesial consciousness and on a refreshing ecumenical awareness, would undoubtedly give new vigor to the evangelical elan with which many young religious pronounce their commitment to the community of goods or "poverty." As Brother Schutz writes: "Let us try to effect a peaceful and continual revision of our means of work and existence, in order to eliminate successively everything that would eventually encumber us or make us secure. Every reserve creates little by little a leaden cloak around us."[23]

The commitment to an evangelical attitude with respect to material goods makes its own contribution to the flexibility and availability of the religious community. The *Rule of Taizé* and its *Spiritual Directives* frequently accentuate the contrast between "boldness" and "store for the morrow," opposing "to live in the present moment" against "to work out projects for the future," "fear of possible poverty" against "a gripping call to live today for God," "man's desire for security" against "living from God's audacity," to "dare to live dangerously" against "the spirit of possession."

It is scarcely necessary to mention that, conceived in

23. Schutz, *L'Unanimité,* pp. 109 f.

this way, the renunciation of private ownership and the abandonment of economic independence that are involved in the commitment to community of goods do not serve to make life easier or to free the religious from cares and a sense of responsibility. The Brothers are kept informed about the community's economic situation and share in the bursar's concerns. As we mentioned before, many of the Brothers work in salaried or independent professions.

Taizé also feels strongly involved in the problem of the "third world" and makes efforts to improve the fate of the helpless people living in these economically underdeveloped lands, both by using its own resources and by interesting others in that fate. As Prior Schutz expresses it:

> At any rate, today the spirit of poverty demands much more than generosity and detachment. Sharing in the miseries of the world is first of all a sharing in the world's struggle against its misery. More than ever before, we are confronted with the question of evangelical poverty in the light of the two-thirds of mankind who live in abysmal wretchedness.[24]

Later we will have an opportunity to return to this economic solidarity with the poor.

24. *Ibid.,* p. 9.

CHAPTER FIVE

CELIBACY

This work of Christ within you demands infinite patience. RULE OF TAIZÉ[1]

THE REVALUATION of Christian celibacy within the tradition of the Reformation is a remarkable phenomenon that draws the attention of both the Catholic and the Reformational Christian. It should be recalled here that it was especially the pledge of celibacy that made Protestants object to the monastic or cenobitic life, whether for mainly emotional reasons or for others based on doctrine, sincerity and full humanity. It is less well known that Calvin himself recognized the possibility of two vocations, viz., to Christian marriage and to Christian celibacy. Christian marriage, too, is not merely a natural and profane concern but also a life of vocation. To accept Christian marriage as a task for life, "for better for worse, for richer for poorer, in sickness and in health, to love and to cherish, till death us do part," can be done only in obedience and availability to God's call. Christian celibacy, as an alternative to the Christian state of marriage, clarifies the vocational character of the latter and restores to it the significance of being a mystery of salvation. Marriage and celibacy have a mutual dialectical relationship to each other in Christianity.

1. P. 48.

One of the theologians of Taizé, Max Thurian, has devoted special attention to celibacy among the three commitments of community life. He deals extensively with it in at least two of his publications.[2] In these works one can distinguish several motivations for Christian celibacy, and the core of these is largely in agreement with what one can find in Catholic works on this question, including the official statements made by Vatican Council II. In the following pages we will examine some of these motives a little more closely; next, we will indicate the relativity of these and all other "motivations"; finally, we will devote our attention to the bond between celibacy and community life as it is seen by Taizé.

1. Availability

Will you, in order to be more available to serve with your Brothers and to give yourself completely to the love of Christ, remain celibate? I will. RULE OF TAIZÉ[3]

The voluntary celibate can go anywhere at any time to respond to an urgent need of the Church. MAX THURIAN[4]

The vocation to celibacy means in principle unlimited availability. The Christian who has this vocation is, as it were, set aside by God, kept free for general service, committed to an availability which *a priori* and of itself knows no limitations whatsoever. The celibate can be put to work anywhere.

From a purely human standpoint, even, celibacy can have a positive significance insofar as it is the expression

2. *Marriage and Celibacy*, London, 1959 (first published in French, 1955); "La Communauté de Cluny," *Verbum Caro*, vol. 2 (1948), pp. 108-124; *Mary, Mother of the Lord, Figure of the Church*, London, 1963.
3. P. 77.
4. *Marriage and Celibacy*, p. 105.

of dedication to a life task that wholly and entirely occupies the individual. His "being free from" is thus being motivated by a "being free for." His unmarried life is not marked by the absence of cares and concerns, but by concentrated care and application.

In marriage one fellow-man demands so much care, love and attention from the other that the wedded we-community would be violated if one of the two were to assume, in addition, a life task whose duties would force him or her to neglect the other.[5] In this sense celibacy can be defended as meaningful not only from a religious standpoint but also on a purely human basis. Availability for exacting tasks in both the Church and the world can demand that one remain celibate. In fact, a high regard for marriage can induce someone to renounce the married state because he considers his total dedication to his life work incompatible with the great demands that marriage would impose on him.

This celibacy, however, becomes unmotivated as soon as the dedication disappears. Its gradual disappearance will slowly make the life of the celibate hollow and sterile. In this way he silently loses his identity and becomes more and more a useless human being. For no one ever finds within himself a reason for a meaningful existence. Willingness to work at something or for someone, availability, sharing and participating with others, dedication and self-sacrifice—these are motives that give lustre and meaning to the life of the celibate. He, too, is not someone who is free but a captive.

Writing to the Christians of Corinth, St. Paul reminded them of the duties of marriage. Those who are married must, according to God's will, take their marriage and family life to heart: "The married man is [and must be]

5. Cf. E. Schillebeeckx, "Het celibaat van de priester," *Tijdschrift voor Theologie*, vol. 5 (1965), p. 307.

anxious about worldly affairs, how to please his wife" (1 Cor. 7:33). Commenting on these words, Max Thurian says: "These human demands of the state of marriage are willed by God, but they are a handicap to a free and unattached service of the Church. . . . Saint Paul stresses the practical advantage of celibacy, since marriage involves of necessity loss of independence."[6]

The Gospel says that he who as a Christian celibate gives up father and mother, wife and children, does so "for my (Christ's) sake and the Gospel," or "for the Kingdom of God's sake." His dedication is not directed to a thing, such as scholarship or scientific research, but to the Person of God and to his fellow-men. He has the mobility of a light-armed soldier and enters God's service for the proclamation of the Gospel and the construction of the world as the City of God. He is not only available for tasks but also at the disposal of persons: "The Christian celibate can always be at everyone's disposal," says Max Thurian,[7] and the same point is stressed by Prior Schutz. In an interview given on the occasion of the twenty-fifth anniversary of the Community's foundation, he expressed himself as follows:

Today, after fifteen years of community life [that is, calculated from the first perpetual vows in 1949], I consider that celibate chastity has opened up for us an ecumenical dimension whose very existence we had not even suspected. Through chastity we want to be men of a single love, a single love of Christ, men so taken up with the hope of God that they wish to keep their arms wide open to everyone and everything, to the all-encompassing, to catholicity, to ecumenicity. . . .

Led us add at once, however, that one who commits himself to celibate chastity can hold fast to it only if he lives in the expectation of God. . . . Thus we must say

6. *Marriage and Celibacy*, p. 106.
7. *Op. cit.*, p. 108.

that a life of chastity can be led only in the spirit of poverty: these two are the guarantees of our orientation to God alone.[8]

This idea of "poverty" and "orientation to God alone" lead us to another aspect of the ideal of celibacy as it was developed by Taizé.

2. *Witness to the Sufficiency of God*

> *The final commitment to celibacy manifests (our) desire to become men of a single love.* ROGER SCHUTZ[9]

In his book about Mary, Max Thurian points to the special value for which a Christian can sacrifice the great good of marriage. He whom God calls to Christian celibacy manifests, by living it authentically, that God is sufficiently great and rich to fill the heart of man. To renounce the fulfilment of life which a fellow-man can give as partner and life-long companion is only the negative side of the profession of God's all-giving and perfectly satisfying fullness. In his own way the celibate gives witness that God is the one to whom ultimately all love refers. By a celibate life man lets it be known that henceforth he expects everything from God, the Creator of all love, and that he absolutely rests on Him. The religious celibate places his human completion and his human fruitfulness entirely in the hands of God.

Thus, celibacy demands that intimate attitude of total expectation based on an absolute confidence in God, the source of all life. Celibacy makes a constant appeal to live in intimacy and union with God. If there is no life of communion with God, of prayerful contact with Him, celibacy would be merely a sign of human poverty and sterile emptiness.

To renounce marriage is to give up a great good. In the

8. *Fêtes et Saisons,* no. 191, 1965, p. 8.
9. *Living Today for God,* p. 99.

eyes of the outsider as well as of the person who renounces it, it means to live in poverty. But this poverty has a splendor of its own, one which it draws from its intimacy with God, from self-surrender to Him. This kind of poverty and beggarliness, willingly accepted in faith, is an incarnation of a genuine trust in God's all-surpassing richness and power. It is a sign of humility and of dependency on God.

It is clear that if celibacy is taken up as a profession of faith in the real and personal presence of God, it renders the religious celibate especially qualified and destined for a life of adoration and worship. In this life of prayer, the celibate not only seeks God but also finds, through his intercession, his fellow-men: "Alone with Christ, he is yet directed, by his status, into frequent dialogue with God, in prayer and meditation, and in liturgical worship of the Lord in the daily office and the Eucharist."[10]

The idea of "contemplative solitude" returns often in connection with celibacy. In his latest book, considered a commentary on the Rule, Roger Schutz writes:

> Any probing of one's own depth leads one to observe that every intimate relation, even for the most united couple, implies limitations. Beyond, there is human solitude. Anyone who refuses this order of nature will know revolt, as a result of his refusal. Consent to this fundamental solitude opens up a way to peace. It lets the Christian discover a dimension, hitherto unknown to him, of his relationship with God. To consent to this solitude, which is a condition of all human life, stimulates the intimacy with Him who delivers us from the oppressive solitude man experiences when he is faced with himself.[11]

And commenting on the words of Christ in the Sermon on the Mount, "Blessed are the pure of heart, for they

10. Max Thurian, *Mary, Mother of the Lord* . . . p. 36.
11. *L'Unanimité*, pp. 126 f.

shall see God," the Prior says: "To remain chaste, to answer the call to purity of heart and to live it authentically—only the desire to see Christ will be able to quench our thirst for intimacy. . . . Only the gaze we keep fixed upon Christ permits a slow transformation."[12] To become pure of heart is the privilege of those who desire to see God.

It is therefore only within and on the basis of unity with God in Christ that one can understand or deepen one's understanding of celibacy. This existential understanding is a gift, for a celibate's balanced life and mature development in celibacy constantly comes from Him to whom he has surrendered himself. Left alone and isolated from Christ, man is not capable of bringing about in himself the harmonious development of his identity. Without inwardness, without search for God, without an always entertained and ever renewed union with Christ, without a "gaze fixed upon Christ," celibacy means boredom, atrophy, the shrivelling away of authentic human life. It is only by living together with God that the religious celibate attains fulfillment of life as a happy and mature man.

The recognition that not he but Christ accomplishes the conversion of his capacity and need for love is an incentive for a deeper life of dialogue with God. It is "Another than self"[13] who transfigures man's affectivity, the human heart and the senses. God's kingly dominion is like the field in which a man sowed his seed. He does not know how and he does not notice it, but the seed sprouts and grows; Christ's work of transformation acts similarly; it is not a sudden push. "This work of Christ within you demands infinite patience."[14]

12. *Living Today for God*, pp. 101 f.
13. Schutz, *op. cit.*, p. 102.
14. *Rule of Taizé*, p. 51.

Christ himself gave the example of such a life entrusted to God. He inaugurated the vocation to celibacy in
His own life. The Taizé Brothers like to refer in this connection to a statement for the celibate life dating back to
the earliest times of post-Apostolic Christianity: "If anyone can live in chastity for the honour of the Lord's flesh,
let him do so without ever boasting."[15] Jesus himself, true
God and true man, made for himself the choice of celibacy for the sake of the Kingdom of heaven. It is the love
of Christ itself that seizes a human being when he responds to the vocation to Christian celibacy.

3. Eschatological Meaning

> *Among Christians who must all use this world as not
> using it to the full, the celibate is a sign of detachment
> required by the expectation of the Kingdom of God.*
> MAX THURIAN[16]

In his first letter to the Corinthians, St. Paul gave the
Christians of that city the following advice: "The appointed time has grown very short; from now on, let those
who have wives live as though they had none, . . . and
those who deal with the world as though they had no
dealings with it. For the form of this world is passing
away" (1 Cor. 7:29-31). Most likely we do not share the
first Christians' idea regarding the chronological nearness
of the end of time; nevertheless, St. Paul's words retain
their validity and actuality. The "worldliness" of every
Christian must be a "holy worldliness," for in its present
form the world bears the stamp of being provisional.

St. Paul's words could easily be taken as of a recommendation to remain aloof from the world, and his counsel could be understood as a kind of camouflaged, "kill-

15. Ignatius of Antioch, *Letter to Polycarp*, **Early Christian
Fathers**, London, 1953, p. 119.
16. *Marriage and Celibacy*, p. 113.

joy" condemnation of human love. On closer inspection, however, Paul does not recommend any negative aloofness or puritanical restriction, but a well-understood dedication. It is not because he has opened the door to "another world" that St. Paul exhorts his Christians to observe a certain distance from a kind of "second rank" world. There is no question of a refusal to serve. If, nonetheless, one wants to insist upon the term "flight from the world," one should speak of a flight into the future, a forward flight away "from a world that does not transcend the 'now' and is limited by what is already in man's grasp."[17]

All Christians must again and again do battle with a world that is in love with itself, a world that wants to "boast of itself." The front lines of this battle lie in man himself. Conceived in this way, the attitude recommended by St. Paul does not weaken the Christian's participation in the world or render it fruitless; on the contrary, it would be more appropriate to speak of disloyalty if one wishes to build the world without this indispensable spiritual co-efficient factor. For the world is a world in evolution and not a world at rest. Whatever is, whatever was and whatever comes to be is an "ascent." Or, expressed in personal terms, God moves all human beings in freedom to the final community, united with Him, the Creator and Restorer. Man's divine sonship and the brotherhood of man are God's design for His creation. Mankind in its completion and fulfillment will be a community, the community of the "saints," that is, of human beings who have authentically become human.

The Christian does his share in the construction of this world-in-the-making by bringing to bear upon it the most profound value of the world and of man, by resisting the

17. J. B. Metz, "Das religiöse Buch," *Stimmen der Zeit*, vol. 176 (1964-65), p. 717.

everlasting tendency of the creature to make itself an absolute and to proclaim its independence from the Source of life. The Christian endeavors to live in the conviction that man does not find the deepest meaning of his life within a world that revolves around itself in total self-sufficiency. By the way he lives he must "make" it true that death is not the end of everything. Thus, his life is at the same time a message presaging the definitive future.

As one whose destiny is linked up with that of his fellow-Christians, the "celibate for the sake of the kingdom of heaven" wishes to give expression in his own way to this eschatological and "evolving" character of life. Through the very way his life is oriented—a way to which his own attitude of life must correspond if he does not wish to live a lie—he reminds both himself and his fellow-men of man's greatness, of the importance of life, and of its far-reaching stakes. The fraternal contribution of the Christian celibate, called by God who also gives him his task, is to draw attention to the fact that he and his fellow-men are not merely dwellers on a planet but really *"laikoi"* (laymen), that is, members of the People of God, a people that now is still "on the way," but that will later be the human community of the final time. His contribution to the world's progress is to make man think of its beautiful completion in its final time; his role is "to make man think of God."

In his own way, then, but together with his married fellow-Christians, he draws attention to the fact that God does not wish to leave the world as it is but wants to raise it to the definitive form willed by Him. At present mankind still lives in the provisional stage. The Christian celibate puts a question mark after the assumed self-evidence of the established and familiar order. He points to the value of the one thing necessary: the fullness and power of God's love which permeates all things and which will fulfill all things in all. In the words of Max Thurian:

> By the commitment to the chastity of celibacy [he] is summoned to become the sign of eschatological newness. . . . He manifests in his status the overturning of the natural creative order by revealing God's invasion in the world and the necessary separation from the things only *of* the earth in order that the fullness of the life in God might have full sway: all is new in creation and human life, for the Lord has come or because He comes. [The celibate] is the living symbol of the ancient liturgical cry: "Maranatha, the Lord is coming."[18]

4. *The Relative Character of These Motivations*

> *We cannot condemn those who do not understand the teaching of Christ on celibacy. He said himself: "He alone can understand to whom it has been given."*
> ROGER SCHUTZ[19]

The attentive reader must have noticed that in the preceding pages we have listened mainly to what one of Taizé's theologians has to say about celibacy. Taizé's Rule itself did not enter into the discussion. As a matter of fact, one would look in vain for a motivation of celibacy in that rule. This silence is a discretion worthy of praise, for it is not on the basis of considering the *pros* and *cons* that one undertakes freely to live one's entire life in celibacy. The vocation to such a life does not depend on the *post factum* attempts a theologian makes to give meaning to it. The motives that can be adduced in favor of celibacy are provisional and permit shifts from one motive to another. The proper and most profound basis of the vocation, however, is unconditional; it does not lie on the side of any particular motivation but beyond all of them. Be-

18. *Mary, Mother of the Lord* . . . , pp. 36 f.
19. *Living Today for God*, p. 95.

cause the true vocation to celibacy is an extreme sign of contradiction in the midst of a sexualized world,[20] it will be appropriate to dwell somewhat longer on this "indefensible" character of the vocation to celibacy.

A vocation is concerned with the whole of the person called, and this statement applies in an eminent way to the celibate state of life. A vocation is a way of learning gradually to understand *oneself*, of gradually beginning to recognize *oneself*, one's appropriate, proper and only authentic, only true *self;* it is a gradual appropriation of one's own identity. And this recognition is encompassed by a growing awareness that everything, and first and foremost, this *self* is a *gift* made by the One who "undertakes" all life. The quiet reflection that is necessary for any genuinely personal life makes man discover that his existence is rooted in a *possibility* which is not at all arbitrary. He can dispose of his life, so he realizes, but he has a destiny. Life, which in the full sense of the term is not just being or remaining alive, but a disposing-of-oneself implies obedience to an *invitation* to be, or rather to become, what one is not yet, and this invitation is not arbitrary but based on a solid orientation. This personal destiny or identity, of which man becomes aware in the form of an invitation, is not delivered one day to him with the morning mail but reveals itself in a discreet way through the life situations of the individual person.

The dialogue in which this "discovery of the self" is accomplished is not limited to a series of passing answers to passing invitations. Man distinguishes himself from the animal in that he looks ahead and, keeping in mind the foreseen interplay of factors governing his life, endeavors to orientate himself by means of a life project. This chosen line gives continuity to his life and thus

20. Cf. *Ibid.*, p. 97.

embodies his faithfulness to the gradual growth of his self.

It is always difficult—we may even say that it is in principle impossible—to account for one's vocation to an outsider. Moreover, it is wrong to ask for such an account, for a vocation is concerned with the deepest being of a person, with his appropriation of the identity that belongs to him alone. On that level one transcends the realm of all "why's." Man's actions can be motivated to the extent that they are objectifiable and, therefore, in principle, repeatable by anyone else with the same effect. However, the more a deed commits the person himself, as is the case when he chooses voluntary celibacy, the more a decision is part and parcel of one's personal vocation, the less any outsider has the right to ask "why." The person is a being expressing self historically and socially and in an embodied fashion; he is unique and irrepeatable; his destiny does not fall under any general category, nor does it correspond to categories agreed upon by a kind of referendum. The answer one would give to an outsider regarding the motive for his vocation would remain unintelligible and unacceptable to him.

The higher and the more demanding a vocation is and the more it involves the whole man, the more difficult it also becomes to account for it with an appeal to motives that are generally accepted. Thus it can happen that a decision determining one's life or the way one wishes to live on the basis of one's response to a personal vocation may appear wholly "gratuitous," unmotivated and irresponsible, to a person who judges that decision from without; yet, at the same time, he who made the decision, the commitment, experiences it not merely as responsible but as a freely accepted "must."

In conversations with others, as well as in reflecting upon it in his own heart, however, it can easily happen that one reasons and argues about his eminently personal response to his vocation as if, after weighing all the pros and cons of many equally valuable and open possibilities, he finally made the choice of this one. He will even try to find reasons to defend this choice. In reality, however, that is not the way in which it came about within himself. Only *post factum* and for the sake of a kind of depersonalized logic—constituted by the current system of generally understood judgments—does he endeavor to clothe his decision with a mantle of public protection by dressing it in "good reasons." But he is very much aware of the fact that there was no question of a genuine competition between a series of juxtaposed possibilities appearing before him as their judge and arbitrator. There was no question of an "impartial" decision, despite the fact that he often tries to base it on motivations that anyone can inspect.

No matter, however, how much the vocation "imposes" itself in this way, it remains, nonetheless, an opting for oneself to become what God wants one to be. This inner "must" that remains helpless before the demand to present legitimate credentials to reason does not do violence to the person; on the contrary, it constitutes the vital power itself of its own identity. The celibate by vocation is just as unable to defend his celibacy as he is to offer a rational explanation of his person. It would be self-estrangement and not emancipation or liberation if one were to abandon his vocation for a "rational motive," to curry public favor or to yield to letters of protest to the editors of the news media. The best service one can render to society undoubtedly is to be oneself. The fact that this does not always make one the most popular member of society only shows that our human scales of values remain merely provisional. It is God who makes the calls, He divides the roles. In a sovereign fashion He decides whom He will call to His community of men and how He will call them. The end of it will be a hymn of praise for His wisdom.[21]

5. *Celibacy and Community*

> One may expect that fraternal life will lead to an unfolding [of the person], to internal freedom because in such a life everything is accomplished in love. ROGER SCHUTZ[22]

Sometimes it seems that, in the eyes of many, the members of Catholic religious orders and congregations are characterized first and foremost by their celibacy. Not-being-married appears to be the primary feature of being-religious. Whatever else may be affirmed of those religious seems to be either deduced from their celibacy or to have a function in relation to it. The strong traditional emphasis on self-sanctification caused great stress to be laid upon individual asceticism. One entered the religious life to strive for perfection, and the primary purpose of this life was often formulated in terms of "self-sanctification." By emphasizing the ecclesial dimension of religious life and its celibacy, Vatican Council II has clarified many things, discarded ill-advised suggestions, and pointed to the right direction.

With respect to Taizé, one could say that, like community of goods and living under authority, celibacy is one of the natural components of religious community life. These three elements of the profession spontaneously call for one another as essential components of the community. We do not mean to say that the community is the final goal of the Brothers' celibate availability. Their entrance

21. In this analysis of vocation we have made use of Roger Troisfontaines' book, *De l'existence à l'être,* Paris, 1953, vol. 1, pp. 335 ff.
22. *Introduction à la vie communautaire,* p. 43.

is not a retreat into the safety of a cloistered ghetto, and the community obviously does not function as a society for celibates. Rather than encapsuling the Brothers in an "introverted" society, the community gathers and orientates their celibate availability. Taizé lives celibacy in a communal way. "Whereas several men could not do much separately, these same men joined together in common life are able to hold on firmly to a faith which can move mountains."[23]

Celibacy provides them with the necessary freedom by which common life and common service become possible. The freedom from the bonds which the state of marriage entails according to God's will, creates the necessary availability without which a true religious community life is impossible. If celibate availability looked upon the community as its final goal, it would betray the mobility of the voluntary single life. The dedicated availability of the individual would die a premature death in an egoistic "we." It is to the Brothers' freedom that the community owes its own flexibility. "They are always on the march, seeking the most dynamic situation in the present time."[24] In this way the community members' elan does not run aground on institutionalization, and their celibacy remains a dynamic factor in a community of service. The dedication of a celibate community is enterprising, open and fertile. Celibacy unites its members, not into a closed circle, but into a missionary community with an "extroverted" orientation.

"For us celibacy obtains its lustre in fraternal love which prepares for true obedience. Like innumerable men today, the Christian suffers mostly from the fact that the expressions of emotional life are choked and repressed—be it that this repression results from legalis-

23. Schutz, *L'Unanimité*, pp. 22 f.
24. Max Thurian, *Marriage and Celibacy*, p. 121.

tic and moralistic sclerosis or from the hardening influence of the events and conditions of life. Community
life with its love of one's fellow-men gives a lustre to all
lawful needs of man."[25] Community life gives to the celibate the family atmosphere that can preserve him from
unwittingly becoming self-centered. It also offers him
friendship and human fellowship, togetherness and
brotherhood, which can help him in the harmonious unfolding of his personality and which may guarantee and
serve the truly human character of celibacy. It stands to
reason, however, that the community does not automati-
cally fulfil that task and provide that help but must strive
to do so.

The thing that can make celibacy a problem is the
daily environment in which one works and lives. Lack of
elementary courtesy and of co-operativeness, glaring ex-
amples of uncharitableness and an absence of the spirit
of collegiality, as well as the institutionalization of life in
an asphyxiating social pattern—those are factors that
undermine celibacy much more efficaciously than the
celibate's inherent weakness and warm-blooded tempera-
ment. The celibate is a vulnerable human being who
needs to experience human fellowship. He neither desires
nor is able to live in isolation. Thus, celibacy does not at
all mean to renounce true human love. Friendship is not
a luxury within a community but a necessity that is
self-evident.

The Christian ideal of celibacy is sometimes objected
to on the ground that "bachelors are just the most selfish,
unaccommodating, particular and arbitrary persons in the
community, while ancient spinsters are the most disa-
greeable, cross, gossiping, and miserable of their sex.
Dreariness unmitigated, a shivering and hungry spirit, a

25. Max Thurian, "La Communauté de Cluny," *Verbum Caro,*
vol. 2 (1948), p. 117.

soul preying on itself, a heart without an object, affections unemployed, life wasted, self-indulgence in prosperous circumstances, envy and malice in straitened ones; deadness of feeling in the male specimen, and impotence of feeling in the female, concentrated selfishness in both; such are the only attributes with which the imagination of modern times can invest" Christian celibates.[26] This reproach still contains a serious warning addressed to all those who have committed themselves to the celibate state of life. They are protected against the danger of the above-described sclerosis only if they devote themselves to a genuine community life and to maintaining an authentic contact with God.

One of the key words of celibate spirituality, as it is pursued by the Taizé Brothers, is the term "transparency."[27] The purity of heart spoken of by the Gospel is connected with this transparency, and the latter evidently is interhuman. He who lives a celibate life must be on his guard against a gruff, stiff reticence and isolationism, as if he were a superman, raised above all human feelings, immune to all temptations. The communal state of life offers him an irreplaceable help in this. "Purity of heart can only be lived in spontaneous and joyful forgetfulness of self in order to lay down one's life for those one loves. This self-giving implies the acceptance of a sensibility often deeply wounded. There is no friendship without purifying suffering. There is no love of one's neighbour without the Cross. The Cross alone makes known the unfathomed depths of love."[28]

26. Newman, *Historical Sketches. The Church of the Fathers*, London, 1873, Ch. IX, p. 167. For celibates it will be very instructive to read the psychological novel of Henry de Montherlant, *Les célibataires*, Paris, 1934.
27. *Rule of Taizé*, p. 52.
28. *Ibid.*, p. 50.

CHAPTER SIX

ACCEPTANCE OF AUTHORITY

There is no hope for a bold and total service of Jesus Christ without unity of mind. Individualism disintegrates the Community and halts its march forward.
RULE OF TAIZÉ[1]

FOR TAIZÉ, the term "authority" is not primarily associated with the idea of "law" or "rule," but with that of "community." It is proper, before one deals with obedience, to keep in mind that we are concerned here not with every type of obedience but only with obedience within a community. "We could say" writes Max Thurian, "that our third commitment, the one that leads to the promise of obedience, is the love of our neighbor. Obedience to God, to the Community, to the Brothers, to the Prior becomes self-evident in the context of love of our neighbor. Obedience without love of our neighbor would appear as a painful restriction."[2]

In the vestry of Taizé there are name-plates above the choir robes worn by the Brothers when they sing the Office. That of the Prior bears the significant legend: *Our Brother.* The Prior has a function within the community, not above it. Life under religious authority has no other

1. P. 55.
2. Max Thurian, "La Communauté de Cluny," *Verbum Caro,* vol. 2 (1948), p. 117.

purpose than being completely at God's disposal. It is one of Taizé's fundamental experiences that the attitude toward God and our relationship with Him have a social, even ecclesial, character. The way God wishes to direct our life is manifested to us within the framework of a society, a congregation, a community. And man's docile availability with respect to that which God expects of him implies, on his part, obedience to an objective, supra-individual direction. As Max Thurian expresses it:

> It is easy to say individually that we obey God. It is also dangerous. Are we not rather obeying ourselves, obedient to our subconsciousness? Or—which is just as bad—do we not interpret everything that is opposed to our own inclination as being surely God's will, out of a kind of self-repression? . . . [By means of obedience] God's will becomes endowed for us with a truly objective character.[3]

For a human being, to live authentically means to go along with God, to let oneself be joined to the human community and inserted in the total order of history. Every life, in a spirit of flexible interplay, participates to some extent in the course followed by the total history of mankind. Thus every life also implies a relationship to Christ, who is The Way. Authentic life, then, is a willingness to follow, with Christ, the God who leads, who goes ahead and initiates His "enterprise." Each one's personal project of life must be a partial project within the total project of God that unfolds itself historically. In the Prior's words, "Christian life places us in the heart of a tension between autonomy and solidarity. It can be lived only in the consent to an inner dialectic."[4] As such, the personal life project essentially is a living of one's voca-

3. *Ibid.*, p. 118.
4. *L'Unanimité*, p. 117.

tion and obedience to it. Moreover, the life in togetherness with others to which God has projected man implies
also that a "group project" or "common creation" will
function as intermediary between each one's personal life
project and God's total project. Man can become himself
only, can be faithful to himself only if, in creative willingness to follow, he goes along with the Lord God and lets
himself be joined to the group project destined for him. If
it is true that we are just emerging from a period of
history and from a culture in which the ideology of individualism strongly predominated, then it will be important
to keep this fundamental truth constantly alive in our
minds.

Let us add that the group, of course, must also manifest the same willingness to follow God in obedience. The
community's faithfulness demands that the group be constantly willing to adapt itself in order to respond to the
questions of the time as they are formulated by God
through the group's situation. In other words, the group
project or "common creation" also must be open, flexible
and willing to go along with God.

Within this community-on-the-way there is an element
which, in function with the historical call encountered by
the community, harmonizes the individual initiatives and
behavior, and this is the authority. Authority arises from
the obedient and available community. Its task is to for-
mulate in a co-ordinating way the answer expected from
the community and to protect it against the contingencies
springing from corrupting and braking factors, such as
moods, the persistent tendency of man to isolate himself
in spite of his destiny for the community, and his endlessly
repeated attempts to renounce his availability. Flexibility is demanded by my insertion in the community God
has destined for me within the Body of mankind that is
the Body of Christ. I am not permitted to identify myself

with my individual insights and initiatives. At every moment my "project," my vision, my initiative must be purified, and it is obedience within the community that offers me the only possible opportunity, the one that is also proper to me. All my initiatives must be conditional, humble and in principle capable of being inserted in the community project.[5] "As regards a project, however suggestive it may be, each Brother should first ask himself this question: Am I always and every day anew united with the common creation and re-creation?"[6]

In Taizé it is especially the community's availability and mobility that calls for the function of the Prior. He is as such a member of the community just as any other Brother. He may not act arbitrarily or in isolation. His authority must serve the community, just as obedience is a serving of the community.[7] Hence it is together with the Brothers that the Prior tries to discover the initiatives and views of the community in order to serve their communal surrender to God's will. The community proceeds collectively in its growth to unanimity with God's will. Accordingly, before considering the Prior and his function, we must first speak about the availability and obedience of the group insofar as these endeavor to find expression in mutual consultation.

1. The Council

The purpose of the Council is to seek all the light possible concerning the will of Christ for the march forward of the Community. Therefore the first step is to

5. I have made use here of J. H. Walgrave's essay, "Kloosterlijke gezagsvoering en geest der gehoorzaamheid," *De raad van religieuze gehoorzaamheid. Colloquium van Magisters,* Tongerloo, 1965 (mimeographed).
6. Schutz, *L'Unanimité,* pp. 116 f.
7. "Autonomous and Solidary" is the title Prior Schutz gives to the chapter dealing with the third commitment in his recent commentary on the Rule, *L'Unanimité,* p. 114.

establish silence in oneself so as to prepare to listen to one's Lord. RULE OF TAIZÉ[8]

In the council each Brother must be orientated to that which God intends for the Community. On that account no votes are taken during its meetings; there is only a discussion of problems: "One does not vote there but speaks." And that speaking has a communal and evangelical ethos. "In the council avoid a tone that brooks no reply, the categorical 'we must.' "[9]

Everyone who takes part in a meeting in which the expressed or unavowed aim is to place the gathering at God's disposal "should come to it not too conscious of his own ideas, but . . . 'heavy with desire' to offer to God one more instrument for Him to use in the world in His own way and in His own time."[10] For common deliberations in which a group endeavors to find its authentic task, an evangelical ethos implies more than the mere recitation of a religious formula for opening and closing the discussions. When life is viewed as guided by God, the meeting will seek God's order of the day. This consciousness of dependence upon God's initiative can bring it about that the over-talkative and the specially dynamic do not seek to dominate and that those naturally reticent are given an equal chance.

In Taizé, the Community does not wait until a unanimous judgment is obtained. The Prior, who presides over the Council, does not only guide the discussion but also the Community. In Taizé, the common deliberations and joint resolutions enjoy a regard that is lacking in many Catholic religious communities. The Prior, however, makes the decisions. If the Brothers' Council presents no unanimity but rather a great diversity of opinions, then it

8. P. 25.
9. *Ibid.,* p. 26.
10. Roger Lloyd, *An Adventure in Discipleship,* p. 58.

is the Prior who makes a provisional decision. "For standing still is disobedience for Brothers advancing towards Christ."[11]

2. *The Prior*

The Prior focusses the unity of the Community. RULE OF TAIZÉ[12]

"To avoid the spirit of seeking to outdo another in argumentation, says the Rule of Taizé, "the Prior is responsible before his Lord for making the decision without being bound by a majority. Freed from human pressures, he listens to the most timid Brother with the same attention he gives to the Brother who is full of self-assurance. If the Prior senses a lack of profound agreement on an important question, let him reserve judgement and, in order to go forward, make a provisional decision, ready to return to it later."[13]

A fundamental difference of viewpoints underlies Taizé's idea of God's guidance and that of the previously mentioned Company of the Servants of Christ the King. The latter assumes that God expresses His will by way of unanimity within the assembly—a standpoint that is not altogether foreign to Catholic Christianity. A general Council of the Catholic Church makes no decisions save by a quasi-unanimous agreement. Nevertheless, Christians of the Catholic or Episcopalian persuasion do not look upon this conciliar or synodal unanimity as the only way in which God's will manifests itself. They ascribe a divinely ordained authority to certain persons in their community. They know how difficult it is to attain unanimity in our human and sinful condition and how often all kinds of inclinations to stand apart or to see one's view

11. *Rule of Taizé*, p. 28.
12. P. 55.
13. *Ibid.*, pp. 27-28.

prevail oppose themselves to God's will. In the *de facto* existing condition of mankind obedience to God often means to overcome oneself, to purify one's own initiative, to give in and to let oneself humbly be inserted in the community's availability for God. It is this view that manifests itself very clearly in the way the Brothers of Taizé speak about the Prior's function:

> Certainly the ideal would be to take no decision that is not a unanimous one. But idealism is not a biblical notion. If we waited for unanimity before moving, the community would very soon become static. . . . Would majority rule on all decisions which affect the community be the best procedure? Doubtfully so, for it would mean the imposition of a method of human society onto the Church. The will of the Lord would have to express itself by fifty-one per cent of the votes. In a community, such a method immediately gives rise to intrigues and politics.[14]

Thus, at Taizé, the function of the Prior is one of unification; he "focusses the unity of the Community." In his book, *Dynamique du provisoire*, Roger Schutz has a chapter entitled "Authority, the Maker of Unity." It is from this standpoint of unity that Taizé views the role of the superior in the community. If the whole community has a vocation to unity and communion, then the function of the Prior serves the same calling:

> He who receives a function of authority is first of all a servant. If he realizes this, he will be on guard against the temptation of paternalism. His service is to stimulate the community, that microcosm of the Church entrusted to him, to strive for unanimity, to be of one soul.[15]

14. Schutz, *Living Today for God*, pp. 115-116.
15. Schutz, *L'Unanimité*, pp. 114 f.

It stands to reason that the Prior can exercise his unifying function only to the extent that his fellow Brothers endeavor to carry out their common vocation to unity. Their application to unity by overcoming individualism is just as indispensable in the community as the unifying endeavors of the Prior. No magic surrounds the latter's function. In the exercise of his ecumenical task and service of unity, the Prior depends on his fellow Brothers' awareness of their vocation and their availability. If this communal consciousness of vocation is insufficiently alive, the exercise of the Prior's ministry of authority can become an occasion for embitterment and divisiveness. For this reason the Rule of Taizé finds it necessary to say:

> The Brothers . . . should recall that the Lord has given a charge to the Prior and therefore give heed to that which concerns his ministry. By their trust, the Brothers renew the Prior in the seriousness of his vocation for the joy of everyone; by a spirit of petty complaint, they paralyse his ministry. Let each Brother, privately, make his fears known to the Prior. Revolt expressed before other Brothers can only contaminate. Satan finds here his best weapon to divide what must be united.[16]

To the extent that a superior[17] is primarily seen as associated with the Rule and the existing established order, he can easily appear to the community not only as the maintainer of this order but even as an "outsider" and

16. *Rule of Taizé*, pp. 56-57.
17. Taizé purposely avoids the use of this term because it could easily suggest that he who has a function of authority is above the others, while he really has a ministry amidst the community. He is the "first Brother," the "Prior." We use the term here, not to reject Taizé's view, but simply because "superior" is the most generally used word to indicate the "head" of a Catholic religious community.

an opponent. His fellow community members, without even being aware of it, instinctively exclude him from the circle of brotherly love and cordiality that unites the community's members to one another. However, according as his function is understood, both by himself and by the community members, as an internal demand of the community itself, he is matter-of-factly included in common fraternal love; hence there really is room then for the superior's rendering of service. He then becomes in effect the "neighbor" who as guide aids his fellow religious. The Epistle to the Hebrews requires Christians not to keep their leaders—and that includes also spiritual leaders—outside their religious attention: "Obey your leaders and submit to them; for they are keeping watch over your souls as men who will have to give an account. Let them do this joyfully, and not sadly, for that would be of no advantage to you" (Hebr. 13:17).

The Rule of Taizé leaves also a healthy room for realism—a point that evidently came up several times for discussion in the Community councils. "Idealism is not a biblical notion,"[18] to which the Rule adds: "The spirit of perfection—if it means imposing one's point of view as the best—is a nuisance to the Community. Perfection is precisely to suffer one's neighbor's imperfection, and to do so out of love."[19] How disarming and therefore conducive to unity would it be if the rules of religious communities were to ask the members to show understanding for the faults and weaknesses of superiors, instead of being dominated by a legalistic mentality! The Rule of Taizé does so explicitly: "The Prior remains subject to the same weaknesses as his Brothers."[20] Such an attitude serves to promote a sense of solidarity between the superior and

18. Schutz, *Living Today for God*, p. 115.
19. *Rule of Taizé*, p. 57.
20. *Ibid.*, p. 57.

his fellow-religious; rather than undermining the community's solidity, it helps establish it on a firm basis.

If it is the Prior's task to "focus the unity of the Community," his office cannot be conceived any longer as primarily administrative or bureaucratic. His main task is to exercise a stimulating, activating, elevating and coordinating influence. "Let him break any authoritarianism within himself. . . . Let him arm himself with mercy, asking Christ to grant it as a grace most essential for him."[21] The Prior's authority is not primarily built on a juridical basis. He will continue to believe to the end in the good will of his fellow-religious. This trust on the part of the superior can become for this fellow-religious, especially when the latter undergoes a crisis, the indispensable starting point from which he may be able to recover his identity as a human being orientated to God.

On the other hand, courage is demanded of the superior. Self-enchantment could induce him to renounce the exercise of his authority and to seek popularity. For this reason the Rule of Taizé exhorts the Prior not "to be weak in the face of pressures on his person. Weakness for him would be the easy way."[22] The service which the community demands of him implies a special kind of self-renunciation. "How can a man exhort and rebuke without being himself a living sermon on self-forgetfulness? Misunderstandings, bitter disappointments, betrayals of all kinds—these are the crosses which must be borne patiently by a man who holds authority in the Church, with a full acceptance of this school of humiliation."[23]

Taizé's Prior did not get his function by way of appointment, nor was he sent by higher authorities to an already established community. He derives his authority most

21. *Ibid.*, pp. 59-60.
22. *Rule of Taizé and Spiritual Directives*, p. 95.
23. Roger Schutz, *Living Today for God*, p. 119.

literally from his charism for building the community. Thus far there has been no question of succession at Taizé. For this reason his function cannot be compared in every respect with the role played by local superiors of communities within a large, international religious society. The latter must not only foster the unity of the local community, but also take care of preserving communion with the other communities of the same religious society. Moreover, they find an order which they themselves did not establish. Their service of the community must see to it that the local group does not isolate itself from its roots and the society's tradition nor from its insertion in a larger whole. At the same time, he must safeguard the community against sclerosis; he is the one who, in the name of God, must foster, encourage and accompany the initiative of the community's members, in order that this community attain the maximum of availability and flexibility. In several respects, then, his role is more difficult. A greater decentralization[24] of authority in those large religious societies can have a good effect on the community's ability to serve and, at the same time, foster the local superior's stimulating and coordinating mission.

In the cenobitic communities that arose after the period of the Desert Fathers authority was not built on a juridical appointment but rather on the charismatic value of the one who was spontaneously accepted as the leader. He was the one sent by God. For St. Benedict, likewise, there was no question of a proper appointment, but the superior derived his spiritual "fatherhood" from a more spontaneous and organic development. For St. Francis of

24. It may be useful to quote here a sentence from Prior Schutz latest commentary on the Rule: "Uniformity creates the appearance of unity . . . Unanimity requires an inner harmony. It implies pluralism of personal expression." *L'Unanimité*, p. 31.

Assisi, finally, the community owed its coherence to "holy fraternal obedience." He did not want any *majores* among his Friars minor, but recommended to the latter flexibility and adaptibility which would enable them, for the sake of the community, to give preference to the viewpoint of their fellow-religious over their own standpoint. Only gradually was the religious superior's position seen in a more juridical perspective.

The practices existing at the beginning of the various periods of religious community life can be useful for the suitable renewal of the religious life desired by Vatican Council II. A renewed reflection on the way a superior obtains his function, on the office he performs in the community and on the attitude the latter assumes with respect to him, as illustrated by modern and ancient founders of religious community life, can perhaps make it possible for us to restore to the superior the charismatic significance that is now more or less obscured: "The superior focusses the unity of the community."

3. Ecclesial Significance

The Brothers of Taizé do not consider themselves an island lying more or less on the fringe of the Church, but living in her very center. The Church's structures and patterns of life are not opposed to that of community life, as if the latter were something eccentric. In this respect religious community life can never claim "exemption." It is precisely in the small concentration of a community, as a "little church," that the ecclesial structures and life patterns of the Church's Body find a clear and eloquent expression. It is possible to discern what the mission and orientation of life in the community ought to be by studying the Body of the Church. And by observing the life of an authentic religious community, one should be able to recognize the figure, the physiognomy and the message of the Church.

In this connection there is a particular theological and ecumenical significance in the fact that the Reformed Community of Taizé accepts the principle that God makes use of men invested with decisive authority in His direction of life. For, does not this fact imply that this community finds itself standing here on a sacramental-hierarchical foundation? And is this principle not a feature of the Church, as she is conceived by Orthodox, Catholic and Anglican Christians, that is discovered here and put to the test by Reformed Christians?

We may conclude this chapter by quoting a sentence from Prior Schutz' latest work: "If the Church demands that there be at the head of each community a man who gives rise to unanimity (and this literally means to have only one soul), a man who gathers together again that which always tends to divide, must she not also accept a pastor of pastors and of communities in order to bring them together again with unremitting care?"[25] And is not this sentence a genuine description of the task pertaining to the bearer of authority in the Church, *viz.* "to be the principle and visible foundation of unity"?[26] If the function of the authoritative office as giving rise to unity could become more clearly visible in its communal significance in the hierarchically structured Churches, its effect, we think, would be gradually to remove one of the most important obstacles to unity among Christians.

25. *Dynamique du provisoire*, p. 102.
26. Vatican Council I, Constitutio *de Ecclesia*, proemium.

CHAPTER SEVEN

COMMUNITY LIFE AND THE RULE

1. *Community Life*

Our fundamental ministry consists in representing the "parable" of the brotherly community and of the unity among men that is possible only in Christ. MAX THURIAN[1]

AND THEY DEVOTED THEMSELVES to the apostles' teaching and fellowship, to the breaking of bread and the prayers. . . . And all who believed were together and had all things in common; and they sold their possessions and goods and distributed them to all, as any had need. And day by day, attending the temple together and breaking bread in their homes, they partook of food with glad and generous hearts, praising God and having favor with all the people. . . . Now the company of those who believed were of one heart and soul, and no one said that any of the things which he possessed was his own, but they had everything in common" (Acts 2:42-47; 4:32).

These words of the Acts of the Apostles form the charter of the Community of Taizé: concentrated attention to the teaching of the Apostles, in meditation, study and proclamation; communion in fraternal openness and mu-

1. "La Communauté de Cluny," *Verbum Caro*, vol. 2 (1948), p. 111.

tual interchange and confession of sins ("one heart and one soul"); and the breaking of the Bread in common prayer.

The perspectives opened by the threefold commitment clearly show that community life does not exist simply for utilitarian purposes, such as team work or a more equitable division of labor. Community life as such is an evangelic witness, it is an existential proclamation and a manifestation of a feature proper to the essence of Christianity, to the Church. Nearly all Reformational communities were born from the discovery that hoarding one's freedom in the sense of an extreme kind of individualism obscures man's outlook on the Gospel and therefore also on God. There is no other Christianity than that within which the idea of community fulfills a vital function.

The proclamation of the Easter message and the announcement of salvation to the world is possible only when the Church is or becomes a true community instead of being merely a gathering in which self-determining individuals make acts of worship. As long as we do not transcend our differences of taste, development, origin and social status in order to unite with one another, we cannot apply the term "Christian" to ourselves; we should not then claim to have a message for the world.

This is the reason why the religious communities consider it their self-evident task to emphasize the communal character of the Church's fundamental structure. The striking gift of Christ is precisely that He "has broken down the dividing wall" that isolates men from one another (Eph. 2:14). What should be typical of Christians is that, whether they be Jews or Gentiles, Greeks or Barbarians, slaves or free men, circumcised or uncircumcised, they find one another in love. This is not always easy, of course, for Christ's gift of unity is also a task.

Thus Taizé also considers its most essential task to

present to the world a "living 'parable' of unity." The Brothers wish to "specialize" in something that constitutes an essential element in the Church's structure and a genuine task for every Christian; *viz.*, to be witnesses, in a torn and individualistic world, to a mutual Christian and human unity that knows how to overcome barriers. By way of this unity and brotherly communion—which is the fruit of commitment and sacrifice—the Christian proclamation will regain its convincing force. "Life in common contains a power of openness to other people. To withdraw within ourselves and turn away from our fellow-men is something that could happen to us, for contemplative life orientates us to inwardness. It could then happen that we would seek only our own personal salvation and forget our fellow-men, our brothers."[2]

"That they all may be one, . . . so that the world may believe" (John 17:21). "That they may be perfectly one, so that the world may know that thou hast sent me and hast loved them" (John 17:23). The Easter message would have been nothing but powerless words and would have failed to make any impression on the world, if this message had not been accompanied by a demonstration of unity, of *community*.

Community, unity is demanded by Christ in order that the world may believe. Hence, by definition, a religious community must be a factor that helps to reduce unbelief and to open the world to the witness of Easter, to its proclamation of reconciliation. Life-in-community is by its very nature a specialization in the Church's fundamental structure, in such a way that those outside the Church can more easily recognize her and desire to belong to her. To live in community is to make the approach to Christ more clearly visible.

Thus, there is no reason to be surprised when one sees

2. Roger Schutz, *L'Unanimité,* p. 13.

that the discovery of the Christian meaning of community has led Taizé to ecumenical service. In reality, the ecumenical vocation is not different from that of being called to religious community. By their very nature religious communities should be in the front lines of the attempts to arrive at unity in the Church and in the world, as well as the attempts to achieve integration and a better economic community among men. That, at least, is the way Taizé conceives its call.

Moreover, the mobility, vitality and unity of mind that are proper to a religious community make it more suitable for experimentation than a large congregation or parish. As a laboratory for the endeavors to arrive at Church unity, the religious community can widen the liturgical and spiritual horizon; and in this way, within the Church and at her service, it can give a new and fresh understanding of dogma, spirituality and even of the Church herself. As we saw, it was in this way that the older Anglican communities worked within their Church. Taizé, likewise, makes a grateful use of that possibility and mission in the realms of the liturgy, of sacramental and spiritual theory and practice. Its influence in these matters radiates far beyond the boundaries of the different ecclesial groups to which the Brothers belong.

Religious communities do not belong in the rearguard of the Church. Wishing to form the rear as a matter of principle is for them a scandalous form of "prudence." They are the vanguard and should act as such. Their unity is not that of a static bulwark, a last redoubt, a closed formation, but the unity of military scouts, flexible and ahead of the rest, for the benefit of the Church. If community life "merely favored purity of life, it would be severely exposed to the danger of dying a slow death. This life demands an ability to adapt oneself to renewals. Those who live this life make use of the freedom given by their condition of being somewhat ahead of the main body of the world and of the Church. Lagging behind would destroy the elan of a life of dedication."[3]

THE HOUSEHOLDS OF THE COMMUNITY

It has been the experience of Taizé that not every situation is equally suited for the best form of community life. Numbers play a role here whose importance should not be underrated. In 1961 the Brothers' council decided that the community members residing at Taizé would be divided into "households" (*foyers*) of about eight Brothers each. The novices, too, were divided into two groups, each with its own novice master.

Although this idea may seem novel, it is really very old. These households are a renewal of St. Benedict's system of *decania*. This system regrouped populous monasteries into smaller "families" of monks, each of about ten persons. It was St. Benedict's wish that these "families" should differ from one another: each should have its own distinguishing features. By means of this very human and wise measure, St. Benedict hoped to counterbalance the weight of big numbers and to avoid their dulling uniformity.

Taizé's *Spiritual Directives* have this to say about these households:

> In common life, the person may sometimes be hindered over a long period of time, by the pressure of the large numbers. It is better then to regroup the Brothers into small living groups or households where mutual fraternal attention recovers its full value. In this way,

3. Schutz, *Dynamique du provisoire*, p. 145. In *L'Unanimité*, Prior Schutz expresses the same idea in these words: "Being too far ahead of history gives rise to feverishness and a spirit of useless contestation, but lagging behind history would destroy the elan of a dedicated life" (p. 14).

too, the meal continues to be this fraternal agape, this time of refreshment of which the Rule speaks.

If we are to use the gifts of each one of us to the fullest, it is important to give a particular responsibility to each household. In the households, a better use can be made of silence, intensifying the contemplative part of our life. But let us keep an absolute discretion in this spiritual experience. There is no particular liturgical prayer in the households, no office outside the common offices of the Community. All Brothers come together for common prayer, the little council in the morning, the evening meetings and for certain meals.[4]

The regrouping of the Taizé Community into six households is done each time for about one year only, lest the larger community disintegrate into merely juxtaposed fractional communities. Each household has its own style, its own initiatives and a special task. For example, in addition to their other work, the members of one group are charged with the reception of guests; another household applies itself especially to sociology, and one of its members comments every day on the relevant news of *Le Monde* and the *New York Times;* a third household dropped one of its meals during Lent—sometimes in agreement with Catholics of the neighborhood—to devote the money thus saved to help underprivileged countries.

Community of life does not first and foremost mean to live under one roof, but implies much more than a purely local bond. Community is possible even if members work or live in different locations. A member of a community who wishes to be a sign of unity can act in accord with the community, even though he is physically absent from it. He only has to see to it that the Prior be at the heart of his initiatives.[5] In the past few years an increasing num-

4. *The Rule of Taizé and Spiritual Directives*, pp. 97-99
5. *Ibid.*, p. 94.

ber of the Brothers have experienced the need to pray from time to time in full seclusion. Taizé offers them an opportunity to do so in a hermitage. Finally, there are the "fraternities." They are not independent houses but provisional establishments outside Taizé that continue to be in constant connection and union with the Community. We will revert to these fraternities in subsequent pages.

2. *The Rule*

Without a rule we risk forgetting our most noble resolutions. It is necessary also to summarize as far as possible a few words from the Gospels in a form which can be easily remembered. ROGER SCHUTZ[6]

These few words express the entire intention and essence of the Rule of Taizé. It may be useful for a study of the function and composition of the constitutions governing Catholic religious orders to sketch here the evolution and the character of Taizé's Rule.

In 1944 Roger Schutz was of the opinion that a rule would lead to a petrifaction of community life: "Not a single statute; not a single rule," he wrote. "It is the Lord of the Church who binds us together in a spiritual unity that finds expression in one maxim [consisting of] three "rules" [that are] one confession of faith. Seen outwardly, those formulas are summary and apply to every Christian. But in the practice of every day they appear to be inexhaustible." These words are followed by the three "rules":

Throughout your day, let work and rest be quickened by the Word of God.

Maintain inward silence in all things, in order to dwell in Christ.

6. *Living Today for God,* p. 55.

Become filled with the spirit of the beatitudes: Joy, Simplicity, Mercy.[7]

These three "rules" are used as "vivifying texts," by means of which one can revitalize himself when the elan begins to diminish.

Nevertheless, Taizé developed not only a series of domestic arrangements, but also a *Rule,* one that retains, however, the three key words Joy, Simplicity and Mercy.[8] This Rule was able to grow and take shape without any constraint or demand from without. It did not have to be a document with which the Community would try to obtain recognition as a moral body in the Church or in civil society; it did not have to satisfy any juridical requirements. Administrative concerns were entirely alien to the conception of this Rule.

Thus Prior Schutz was able to limit himself to putting the evangelical ideal in a form that would readily bring to mind the essential lines of the religious vocation and the contours of the evangelical impulse. Although in 1944 there was not yet question of any developed Rule, the Prior even then made the following remark concerning the value of some kind of schematization for the spiritual life:

How would it be possible for us to subject all the elements of the problem [facing us in more difficult moments] over and over again to examination? . . . To give an example, What rule ought a scrupulous man to impose on himself? First of all, to make a radical break with anxiety as soon as it appears on the horizon . . . . The second element of his rule could be

7. Schutz, *Introduction à la vie communautaire,* Geneva, 1944, pp. 22 f.
8. "Our Rule centers around three words which we would like to engrave in the very stones [of our community] and in all our attitudes." Interview of Prior Schutz with Jean Guitton, *Le Figaro,* 21-22 *Jan.,* 1961.

stated as follows: to abandon myself to Christ alone because everything works for the good of those who love Him."[9]

The positive value of a *Rule* the Prior also described in terms of getting rid of a wasteful irresolution. The Preamble of the Rule says: "Far from groaning under the burden of a rule, rejoice; for, as you renounce all thought of looking back and are borne forward together by the same Word, each day anew you are able to throw yourself towards Christ."[10] It is an old established idea that the lack of bonds rather than the possession of them makes man a slave. Let us explore this idea a little. There are many people who do not go beyond diagnosing their situation. But, no matter how sharp one may be in such an analysis, it is of no great account if one compares it to the decision to put an end to such deliberation and to set out along one particular road. "One particular road," that means, not to undertake things as they happen to strike us from one day to the next, but to live with foresight and care for continuity and interconnection. A radical lack of self-commitment is the most serious obstacle to becoming fully and maturely human and a perfectly camouflaged form of the refusal to accept an authentic identity. At a given moment, one has to set a course and provide one's life with an over-all continuity. The Rule's function is to help man in this matter:

> When a man who has committed himself for life passes through a period of tensions, he is tempted to ask himself whether on the day of his definitive commitment he did not lack clear foresight. But, who ever possesses completely the necessary lucidity to be resolute? Man comes to know successive lucidity throughout

9. Schutz, *Introduction à la vie communautaire,* p. 86; cf. *Living Today for God,* p. 55.
10. *Rule of Taizé,* p. 55.

his entire existence. If he wanted to wait for complete clarity before taking an option for life, his whole life itself would not be enough. There would no longer be an act of faith. Christ alone transfigures that which, at the beginning, was obscure and unfinished.[11]

It is true that mere prohibitions can have negative results. If we do not immediately add something that is positively stimulating to the warning, the latter could produce discouragement rather than encouragement. Moreover, the Rule should present the evangelical elan in an encouraging fashion to those who pass through difficult times.

Taizé's official Rule was published in 1953. It is expressed in the second person singular, for it wishes to speak and address an appeal. It does not begin with the description of the Institute's purpose and its juridical position within the Church. There is no description at all but merely a call:

> Brother, if you submit to a common rule, you can do so only for the sake of Christ and the Gospel. . . .
> Common impulse will stimulate your interior discipline which is so essential for your life as a Christian. From now on you are no longer alone. In all things, you must take your Brothers into account. . . .

After this introduction the Prior speaks about the function and significance of a rule of life:

> You fear that a common rule may stifle your personality, whereas its purpose is to free you from useless shackles, so that you may better bear the responsibilities of the ministry and make better use of its boldness. Like every Christian, you must accept the tension between the total freedom given by the Holy Spirit and the im-

11. Schutz, *L'Unanimité*, pp. 103 f.

possibilities in which you find yourself due to your neighbor's and your own fallen nature.

You would narrow your understanding of the Gospel if, for fear of losing your life, you were to spare yourself. Unless a grain of wheat dies, you cannot hope to see your own self open out in the fullness of Christian life.[12]

The Rule contains only directives of spirituality. It does not stipulate such an item as how much money a "fraternity" is permitted to spend without referring to the Prior; it is silent about eligibility for offices or functions, personal "trousseau," funerals, periods of greater or lesser silence, endowments, precious objects, the duration of night's rest, pigeon holes for mail, impediments for admission, indemnities, permission to hunt, secularization, inheritance, annual reports and budgets, rules of precedence, flight from the monastery.

Taizé's Rule has the following chapters:

1. The Acts of Common Life: Prayer, The Meal, The Council, Order
2. The Spiritual Discipline
3. The Vows
4. Brothers on Mission
5. New Brothers
6. Guests
7. Conclusion
8. Exhortation Read at the Profession

The Rule concludes as follows:

There is a danger in having indicated in this Rule only the minimum necessary for the common life. It is better to run this risk and not to confine oneself to complacency and routine. . . .

If this Rule were ever to be regarded as an end in itself and to exempt us from ever more seeking to dis-

12. *Rule of Taizé*, pp. 9, 12, 13.

cover God's design, the love of Christ, and the light of
the Holy Spirit, we would be imposing on ourselves a
useless burden. Then it would be better never to have
written it.[13]

It was a wholesome thought to keep juridical and
domestic matters outside Taizé's Rule of life. After all,
one lives by the Gospel message as it is proclaimed and
put into focus by a founder or in a rule of life. The
consideration of juridical or moral "cases" and definitions
concerning the domestic conduct of affairs evidently have
only a secondary character. In no respect can they replace the dynamic and spiritual impulse by which a community tries to live. Watchfulness over this spiritual rule,
in addition to the warning that a custumary must always
remain adaptable and has only a subordinate value, are
the best safeguard against petrifaction. The latter will
show itself very easily when one attempts to place the
evangelical inspiration of life on the same level as juridical arrangements.

NOTE ON THE JURIDICAL ELEMENT IN THE LIFE OF A
RELIGIOUS COMMUNITY

It is inevitable that in the older Catholic religious communities the question about the meaning and value of the
juridical element will impose itself with increasing ur-
gency. These communities date from an era in which a
juridical status was a necessary condition to be recog-

13. *Rule of Taizé*, pp. 67 f. Until 1966 in between these two
paragraphs there was the following reference to a customary: "The
Customary defines certain requisites of the common life and of
the ministry according to the time and the need. It must remain
very concise and always subject to revision. Otherwise it would
soon stifle the Rule and place us again under the law." This
passage has now been dropped from the Rule. As a matter of fact,
Taizé has never composed a customary.

nized in the Church and in society. The clear descriptions and definitions which marked the constitutions of many religious orders and congregations did render good service and gave these institutes an administrative identity. The juridical element is something unambiguous, which makes it easy to survey and handle the whole. This element was not an invention of the founders of orders and congregations: they were original and dynamic human beings heading new available communities. To a large extent the juridical framework was imposed on the latter by the period and the society in which they lived. And this legal framework failed to capture or express the inspiration of these founders. Generally speaking, it was their successors who, faced with an ever increasing task of administration and coordination, embodied their concern for the community entrusted to their care in those clearcut and easy to understand definitions and descriptions. The elan that animated the founders and their first followers was something undefinable and incomprehensible if we compare it to these clear canons and practices.

It would be a sign of a false spiritualistic tendency if one were to think that juridical rules are entirely superfluous. Just as man needs some kind of a home if he wishes to dwell somewhere, so also does he need in society certain mutual understandings and regulations in which his bond with his fellow-men and his collaboration with others can become visible, grow and be protected. The absence of any domestic agreements or of financial regulations would be just as damaging to society and to a religious community as a situation in which they are caught in a welter of regulations that have become or are in the process of becoming autonomous and inflexible. Regulations are useful as long as they serve, but not when they dominate. They should remain subject to modification, to being disposed of, and should be regarded as relative; they may not impose themselves as inviolable, absolute and transcending time.

On the other hand, it does not belong to the individual one-sidedly to modify the existing agreements or to cast aside common regulations. For his loyalty to the society or community embodies itself also in respect for this framework of regulations. It is the society or community itself that must constantly reflect upon the usefulness of its own juridical rules, instead of slavishly surrendering to them. Petrifaction can be prevented only if the society constantly checks the suitability and flexibility of its laws.

In that case, the codification of customs and agreements is a good and contributes to the building of the society or community. Today, however, it seems to be time also to become aware of the excessive value attached to the juridical dimension by many religious institutes. Much would be gained if these institutes could reduce this swollen legal dimension to the relative and functional significance it is entitled to.

In Catholic novitiates it has long been the custom to devote the greatest possible care to making aspirants familiar with the particular set of laws and rules governing their order or congregation and to explain these constitutions in great detail. Thus a heavy religious emphasis was placed on the novice's orientation to rules and regulations that were largely administrative and of domestic concern. True, the novices were always told that the fundamental ideas underlying their religious life came from the Gospel and not from those constitutions. Nevertheless, far more time and effort were devoted to these than to the scriptural inspiration of religious life.

In addition to the constitutions, much care was often also devoted to a study of canon law for religious. Nothing was left to chance here, and an examination had to deliver the proof that the novice was familiar with the law. The novitiate was rightly regarded as a period for laying foundations, but the juridical dimension often constituted a disproportionate share of this foundation.

It could happen that it was left to chance whether or not every novice had a copy of the Bible, but the novice master saw to it that each one had a copy of the constitutions. Losing one's copy of the latter was sometimes regarded as almost a kind of sacrilege. The idea that one made his profession on these constitutions existed and was even encouraged. In this way one can understand that the commitment by which one wished to entrust himself to God and to devote his life to Him within the bond of a fraternal community, assumed the appearance of a legal deed. Yet the novice master would quite honestly try to keep alive the suggestion that the congregation's book of laws and regulations summarizes the spiritual elan and the evangelical inspiration which animates the life of religious availability within the bond of the community.

It may be appropriate to illustrate, by means of certain analogous situations, that the privileged position of the juridical element in the novitiate is not as "natural" as it looks to those who are accustomed to that state of affairs—and that includes also official visitors and religious superiors.

Let us look at the case of two young people who prepare themselves for marriage. Anyone would be greatly surprised if they should discuss all the time the civil code of laws covering divorce, alimony, inheritance, adultery, legitimization of offspring, and, in addition, the Church laws governing bans, *sanatio in radice,* impediments and their classification, separation from bed and board, times closed for solemn weddings, etc. Imagine, finally, that, on their wedding day, the couple would give each other copies of the civil and canonical law books governing their married status. One would rightly conclude that these two misguided spouses suffer from a peculiar form of narrow vision. It is true, of course, that a normal preparation for marriage should include a juridical element; nevertheless, the place of the latter must be minor. Its role should not be the main topic of reflection and discussion during the period of preparation; its place in the marriage ceremony should be discreet and unobtrusive. It is only in a time of crisis that the juridical dimension makes itself felt.

Similarly, when a priest helps a non-Christian prepare for being incorporated in the Body of Christ which is the Church, it would be very strange if he were to speak extensively about such matters as the right of patronage, sequestration, irregularities, stole fees, foundations, cemeteries, the conferring of benefices, the alienation of ecclesiastical goods, the expense of canonical litigation, the irremovability of pastors, *vicarii oeconomi*, vindicative and medicinal penalties. The convert would be very much surprised if his baptism and incorporation in the Body of Christ were accompanied by the gift of a copy of the Code of Canon Law, or if he was urged to study this book very carefully in preparation for his baptism. For the liturgy does not invite him to pronounce his baptismal promises on this code of law. While the convert is expected not to reject this collection of agreements and regulations, the liturgy of baptism does not consider it necessary to emphasize this expected loyalty.

The autonomy and absolute character ascribed to the juridical dimension in some religious communities appears to contain a danger of formalism and petrifaction. The mobility and availability that existed at the founding of a community or in its new members at the time of their entrance can easily become paralyzed if the significance of domestic regulations is overestimated; those dispositions are then replaced by static immobility, self-satisfaction and the extinction of enthusiasm. In Taizé, the Brothers devoted much reflection to the "dynamics of the provisional," which offers greater freedom and more availability to the degree that one is more faithful to the essential. It may be useful to repeat to oneself the invitation of Taizé's Prior:

> In the strong current of contemporary history it becomes more urgent than ever to consider, all of us together, our common life in its essence and to actualize in it that which it ought to be. By its very nature, all life in community is orientated to God and to men. If [community life] favored only purity of life, it would run the risk of dying a slow death. [Community life] demands a capacity for adaptation to renewals. . . .
>
> Today, more than ever, if community life nourishes itself with the sap that is proper to it, if it fills itself with the freshness of fraternal life that distinguishes it, it becomes in the Church and for the world a powerful ferment, capable of lifting mountains of indifference and bringing mankind an irreplaceable taste of the presence of Christ.[14]

APPRECIATION OF MOBILITY

> *The spirit of poverty, the sense of the provisional, the "today" of the Gospel are indispensable for the Institution in order that no one deprive us of the freshness of the Gospel.* ROGER SCHUTZ[15]

From the very beginning Taizé has been characterized by its high regard for mobility and willingness to be adaptable. As early as 1946 Maurice Villain noted that this characteristic was the fascinating dimension of

14. *Dynamique du provisoire*, pp. 144 f. The last paragraph of this quotation was also contained in the letter of thanks which Prior Schutz addressed to all religious on the occasion of the inauguration of The Church of the Reconciliation.

15. *L'Unanimité*, p. 66.

Taizé, that the Community was "fully involved in the search for its formula" and that "it did not refuse anything that could make it better."[16] This openness to the provisional, as we saw, was not viewed as the inevitable inconvenience of any beginning. On the contrary, it is an indispensable element of a living organism—to such an extent that one can say that the degree of viability possessed by the living body which any community must be is determined by its greater or lesser power of adaptation. A man like Cardinal Newman was very sensitive to this "law." In a conference he gave, at the age of seventy-seven, to his confreres of the Oratory which he had founded, he said:

> Our congregation is now entering on its normal state. To be ever one and the same, to be ever changing, both together, one as much as the other, is its normal state. . . . It is by change that it perpetuates its identity. . . . When once it has the experience of the second element of its identity, it can never be loose of it again. This is the state of our Congregation, my dear Fathers, on which we have now entered; henceforth change is an element of our existence.[17]

The very title of Roger Schutz' work, *The Dynamism of the Provisional,* speaks in very clear language of this matter. I cannot resist the temptation to conclude this chapter with an excerpt from this book, in which the Prior pleads for mobility as an attitude of life that is urgently needed by the Christian, especially if he has communal responsibilities:

> He who lives in the provisional sees his march toward unity reactivated, for the greatest threat of all would be

16. "La Communauté de Cluny," *Irenikon,* vol. 19 (1946), p. 165.
17. Quoted by Meriol Trevor, *Newman. Light in Winter,* New York, 1963, p. 538.

to be sufficient unto ourselves, to put a discovered treasure under lock and key, . . . and then to institute, for future centuries, structures which would quickly become factors of isolation. . . . The history of Christendom shows so many institutions which, in order to last through time, gave up the provisional character of their beginning! In this way the horizon of those who belong to them was narrowed down. They can survive only by withdrawing behind protective barriers.[18]

To preserve stereotyped forms is making a mockery of tradition; to become static means that the community is deprived of its power of communication.

18. *Dynamique du provisoire,* pp. 151 f.

PART THREE

ECUMENICAL VOCATION

Be a ferment of unity. Never resign yourself to the scandal of the separation of Christians.

Be consumed with burning zeal for the unity of the Body of Christ. RULE OF TAIZE[1]

1. P. 44, and Preamble, pp. 15-16.

Introduction

During his life every human being is on the road toward his own true self. His task is to become more and more the man whom the Creator has in mind and wishes to create; God is the Creator of self-realizing man; His creative action does not stop with man's birth but remains active during the entire path stretching from man's birth to the moment when he changes his temporal condition for his definitive state.

God is not exclusively occupied with the individual, however. Through His creative action which is formative of man, God also is occupied with the creation of a community of men. "All men become brothers"—that is God's design, the goal of his creative work. He does not passively watch either the authentic coming-to-be of man or the establishment of an authentic human community. Not only does the entire plan come from Him, but He Himself gives rise to the personal, self-unfolding human life, as also with his own hands He forms the growing communal Body of mankind.

Unfortunately no one is the man he ought to be, for all are unfaithful to their Creator and to their unique life task. Thus the human community of love, likewise, is a task that has always been constantly betrayed and unfulfilled. Instead of union and communion, there are separatism and lack of love.

Scripture mentions all this explicitly in explanation of the Incarnation and Mission of Jesus Christ. In the midst of a failed humankind, He is the first and the only one who unreservedly yielded to God's creative activity. In a world of separatism and divisiveness, He is also the perfect fellow-Man. "Christ Jesus is our peace, who has made us one, and has broken down the dividing wall of hostility, . . . that he might create in himself one new man in place of the two, so making peace, and might reconcile us to God in one body through the cross, thereby bringing the hostility to an end" (Eph. 2:14-16).

We are not far from the truth when we say that within the Creator's design it is the intention of Christ to bring reconciliation. The mission and the power of Christ, and therefore also the task of Christianity, is to be the leaven which the Creator took and hid in the world until the latter is totally permeated with it. Christ is, and the Christian should be, a ferment of unity. His heart-felt prayer is: "that they all may be one."

The idea of unity, which is the core of the Christian mission in the world, has acquired in our time a kind of ally in man's social and technical evolution. The communication media make mankind increasingly more uniform. The newspapers of the world depend on the teletypes of half a dozen international news agencies. Television reaches increasingly larger areas with the same programs. Man's way of dressing tends to become standardized. The same is happening to his dwelling, furniture, utensils and even his food. The phenomenon of urbanization is world-wide. Finally, there is an increasing multiplicity of international contacts, congresses and workshops.[2]

Christianity tries to adapt itself to this development toward unity, not as an unprincipled drifting along with the trends, but because it is aware of its mandate and sensitive to the situation. Christians can find inspiration and support in their awareness of their own mission. For the present social and technical evolution also reveals more clearly than ever before the discriminating and disintegrating tendencies existing in the society of mankind. It is obviously necessary to take a stand with respect to the tide of evolution, for simply drifting along in the

2. Cf. *Aujourd'hui, Journal de Taizé,* No. 4, Oct., 1963, p. 3.

stream of events does not lead to harmony and reconcilation but to destruction and disintegration.

It has been given to the Christians of our time to see the unity intended by Christ no longer primarily as a gift already made, or as a static uniformity, but as a dynamic communion to be realized. The Community of Taizé was able to make a grateful use of this ecumenical climate that extended a welcome to it at its birth. From the very beginning the idea was alive at Taizé that the Community could only in a defective fashion respond to its vocation if it were to turn its tendency to unity exclusively inward, if it were to limit its task to fostering fraternal love only among its own Brothers. A religious community is authentically itself only to the extent that it acts as a leaven of unity in this world. In conformity with their project to be a living parable of unity, therefore, the Brothers endeavored to permeate themselves with a vigorous ecumenical tendency. In the twenty-five years of their existence, they have developed an ecumenical spirituality which richly deserves to be studied and practised.

CHAPTER EIGHT

ECUMENICAL SPIRITUALITY

To be ecumenical requires application. Sometimes one meets people who think that an ecumenical mentality is a spontaneous gift of youth or that one can acquire it without effort. True, there are men for whom the term "ecumenical" has degenerated into more or less of a fad or an accepted form of being polite to dissenters. Others simply like to play with "being ecumenical." But to be truly ecumenical is just as difficult as being a Christian; it demands unceasing efforts and a constant reflection on one's own way of acting. The touch stone of an authentic ecumenical attitude may perhaps be sought in one's conduct with respect to oneself and those of one's household.

The first prerequisite for union or reunion with others is the establishment of unity and harmony within oneself, that is, agreement of thought with deeds, of being with acting, consistency with the best and the deepest within oneself.[1] Embitterment and self-pity are factors leading to disintegration and isolation. Concerning these destructive forces Roger Schutz recently wrote: "In regret the interior man disintegrates. Instead of being toned up, the spirit of man becomes sterile when he is dragged down into a reflection in which he reconstructs, without

1. Cf. Schutz, *L'Unanimité*, p. 29.

benefit, a situation that is past. Regret makes the creative elan sterile. Regret makes it weak."[2]

It is on the basis of this inner unity, of peace with, and loyalty to himself that one can live in a society as a unifying factor. In connection with this, Prior Schutz remarks:

> Unity among Christians therefore presupposes that we are agreed upon the necessity of each man being at one with himself. This unity of the person cannot be set aside without serious consequences. . . . Unity of the personality presupposes a man's fidelity to his initial solemn promises so that on every occasion he is able to take upon himself his big personal decision.
>
> No good is done however by our hiding from the fact that the unity of the person has been destroyed by the "Separator," the "diabolos"—the Devil. . . . Man, divided in himself, is divided too in his relations with his neighbor. Because he lacks this personal unity there quite often arises from the very depth of his personality the need to assert himself against someone else—the need to separate what should be united. So too Christians set themselves in opposition to other Christians, sons of the same Father—and they do this sometimes with all the justification of a confessionally good conscience![3]

1. Unity at Home

If we want to call all Christians to visible unity, let us begin with ourselves, realizing unity daily within ourselves and among ourselves. SPIRITUAL DIRECTIVES[4]

The Brothers of Taizé represent twenty autonomous Churches and, in addition, many different national mentalities. They come from Switzerland, France, Germany, Great Britain, Holland, Scandinavia and the United

2. *Dynamique du provisoire,* pp. 175 f.
3. Schutz, *Unity Man's Tomorrow,* New York, 1962, p. 17.
4. *The Rule of Taizé and Spiritual Directives,* p. 101.

States, and they belong to Lutheran, Reformed, Presbyterian, Congregational and Episcopalian Church communions. Concerning the road to unity within the Community, Prior Schutz made the following remark in an interview:

> We learn to make progress toward unity first of all by common prayer and by living together in friendship. Liturgical prayer is a means that forms that doctrinal unity which is elaborated in the novitiate. We discover together, and together we bring to maturity common themes, the important themes.
> Are you a kind of school of unity?
> No, not a school. We would rather like to give a kind of living testimony to the scandalous nature of division, [and be] a gathering that makes one put the finger on the intolerable aspect of that division.[5]

Taizé's experiences in this matter agree with those of the Anglican communities of the nineteenth century: liturgical life gives a more profound insight into faith and operates toward doctrinal harmony. Nevertheless, each of the Brothers remains faithful to his own Church communion. Their togetherness in the Community does not negate the Christians' dividedness, but their firm solidarity constantly, as it were, shows how intolerable that dividedness is.

Because of man's fallen nature, ecumenism, as well as this living together in community, will always mean reconciliation and reunion. "Ecumenism always begins with this reconciliation of man with God, and then of man with man, in the family, in his profession, in his surroundings. It is only from these short-range reconciliations that it will be possible to set out toward that grand universal reconciliation of all of us in one Church."[6]

5. Interview with Sammy Chabrillan, *Panorama chrétien.* July, 1963, p. 21.
6. *Fêtes et Saisons,* Jan., 1965, p. 24.

In a family or community unity is never an unbroken unity but always a regained, a recovered unity. Brotherly love is never an idyllic romanticism but honest realism. Before joining the ecumenical movement at large, the Christian who wishes to be authentic first tries to live and cultivate unity "at home." The true ecumenical attitude, which wants to be more than a passing gesture or a fashionable pose, finds its training grounds in its own backyard. To be a factor of unity one need not wait until he meets someone of a different persuasion. How could one dare to present himself "for the service of unity" if he is not really willing to serve the same cause at the place where it ought to be served foremost; *viz.*, at home? The lack of sincerity with which such a person lays claim to the title of being ecumenical can only do harm to the cause of ecumenism. It would be a modern form of the hypocrisy, the religious play-acting, against which Jesus Christ reacted so strongly in the Gospel.

Brother Robert, the physician, formulates this necessity of "home training" in unity as follows:

> Community life is a school of unity, a school of dialogue. And the demands of the ecumenical vocation are pressing: before we dare to speak about the unity of Christians, we learn that unity must be profoundly lived in the nearest Christian family, that is, for us here, "the Church of God at Taizé." And we know in a very concrete way what is meant by fraternal love, pardon, respect and consideration for one another.[7]

The idea of reconciliation as the first and most universal requirement for any form of *rapprochement* has become almost an institution at Taizé. The newly built church is called The Church of the Reconciliation. At its

7. *Aujourd'hui, Journal de Taizé*, No. 8, Oct., 1964, p. 5.

entrance, a large sign invites all visitors to reunion, in French, English and German:

ALL YOU WHO ENTER HERE
BE RECONCILED
THE FATHER WITH HIS SON
THE HUSBAND WITH HIS WIFE
THE BELIEVER WITH THE UNBELIEVER
THE CHRISTIAN WITH HIS SEPARATED BROTHER

This church has become a shrine of pilgrimage. All kinds of people who live in dividedness and are unable to restore unity come to this church. They bring their intentions, intentions of reconciliation: to heal a broken home, to restore harmony between two human beings, to render peace to our family.

In addition to the task of forming a single community composed of men belonging to different nations and denominations, Taizé also faces the duty of living a life of unity between two generations. The first Brothers are close to fifty years old, the youngest are in their twenties. The Community has already duly noted this internal ecumenical task—which is always a prerequisite for a task's fulfillment.

As a matter of fact, the whole of human society faces this same task. In our time of rapid change and development, there often is tension between the older and the younger generation, and this tension poses a challenge to an authentically ecumenical attitude. At present, everything seems to be undergoing a revaluation. Much of what the older generation learned in its youth reveals itself as out of touch with today's levels of knowledge and appreciation. Thus, what is needed now is a constant willingness to adjust the course, much patience and great mildness of judgment. Only "a daily renewed application of the mind," says Prior Schutz, "allows constant renewal and adaptation to the new trends. Only minds that do not work become rusty." And "To grow old out of touch with the upcoming generations is to condemn oneself to vegetate. . . . The most dangerous enemy is the divorce between generations. Everyone runs the risk of losing everything in it: the younger generation that of profiting by the human and spiritual experiences of their elders; the less young and the older generation that of being relegated to a situation in which they can no longer live but have merely to wait passively for death."[8]

In addition to the tension between generations which gives tone to the constantly renewed realization of unity, there are tensions arising from divergent initiatives. Especially if a community is composed of artists, theologians and other academically trained people, there exists a temptation to free-lancing which could endanger the insertion of the individual's work in that of the community and make him pursue his aims in isolation. "In every community," writes Prior Schutz, "it is every member who, day after day, participates in the re-creation of the entire body. If a member, under the impulse of a personal creative passion, accomplishes his work without inserting it in the common creative activity, he unwittingly does destructive labor. There is no community life unless the one and only reference point of all is to build together. The sign of unity which in that case will radiate among men is more important than the noblest of all individual work."[9]

Thus, ecumenism "at home" is a task that belongs to all. It is perhaps the most difficult of all and never fully realized. At the same time, however, it is also the best contribution to the ecumenical movement. Writing from

8. *Dynamique du provisoire,* pp. 31-32 ("Consentir l'aujourd'hui").
9. *Dynamique du provisoire,* pp. 49 f.

Rome, where he was then observing at Vatican Council II, Prior Schutz told his fellow-Brothers:

> From here I see Taizé as a very small light. . . , the light of Christ shining in your midst. This light is, as it were, surrounded by a halo of peace and fraternal love. . . . To live unity, peace is needed. There is no unity without peace. In addition to peace, I see love, which finds expression among you in fraternal attention. [Love is] to have all the time for the other the same regard as for Christ, to be attentive to him, to refuse to build for oneself a little niche in the common life in order to live there a personal existence without genuine presence to one's own brother, one's nearest neighbor.[10]

2. *Solidarity with One's Own Church*

> *To venerate the mystery of the Church, to consent to our impossibilities in the face of certain burdens, that means to be able, if need be and at the opportune time, to beg, pray, exhort and permit that "the event" burst open in the bosom of the institution without, however, breaking its unity.* ROGER SCHUTZ[11]

One of the cheapest procedures of a so-called ecumenical attitude undoubtedly is an unlimited willingness to negative criticism of one's own Church. Every Church, of course, offers plenty of material for an examination of conscience. But an ecumenism that despises one's own Church is of a low grade. One may think that in this way the favorably impresses his separated brother, for quite often the motive of such an attitude lies in a self-defense based on a strong feeling of insecurity. Most of the time, however, the separated brother is merely shocked by this unprincipled egocentric exhibition.

Speaking about Christian unity, about the *aggiornamento* which every Church community must undertake in order to arrive at this unity, Roger Schutz often refers

10. *Fêtes et Saisons*, Jan., 1965, p. 13.
11. *Dynamique du provisoire*, p. 98.

to St. Francis of Assisi. In his days there existed an abundance of reasons for bitter reproaches to the Church and to break away from solidarity with such a defective ecclesial family. St. Francis the reformer, however, did not choose the road of open or camouflaged schism; yet his solidarity and humility bore much fruit.

Today one can hear many objections to the institutionalized character of the Church and, it must be admitted, many of these objections are solid. Some people, however, in their disappointment and embitterment, think that any form of institution is *per se* a deformation of the human ideal and above all of Christ's mission. Thinking that they are faced with the dilemma, either the institution or "event," they opt for the latter and radically reject the former.

In one of his works Prior Schutz puts down a number of reflections regarding this matter, reflections which undoubtedly reached maturity in the course of years within his community. He begins by pointing out that one or the other form of the institutional dimension is indispensable: "The institution is an environment in which, generally, we find ourselves placed by our birth. It is often a great handicap for our relationship with Christ and the Church. It is as if the institution loads us down with an almost unsupportable burden and threatens to asphixiate in us that evangelical freshness which characterizes the Christian."[12]

One would like to get rid of it. Yet, if we are "available" men, God can gradually lead us to the realization that not separation but a more intense spiritual life is able to renew the Church:

To consent to the Church's institutions, to become solidary with them, is to become really able to be the ferment in the dough. When a leaven is truly a ferment,

12. *Dynamique du provisoire,* p. 93.

what a power does it possess to raise the dough and to burst open the crust that constantly forms again on aging institutions! Nothing can resist such a leaven.

Reacting to the ponderous weight of an ecclesial body can be necessary to renew in it that which is falling into ruins. But if those who express this reaction become as it were professional protesters and if, in addition, they reorganize themselves in groups and shout from the outside, then they succeed merely in blockading institutions that are already tired by a long life and in preventing their reform.[13]

There is an eternal temptation to try to live a Christian or human ideal in complete freedom from every institutional dimension. When a Church splits, "spiritual-minded" members have often thought that they could do without the institutional character and have turned away from the organized Church body. Soon after their separation, however, they reorganized themselves within an institutional framework. The end result of their entire effort to purify Christianity was nothing but a multiplication of the number of Church institutions. The taints affecting the institutional dimension can be removed only from within. Every institution needs such an unending reform. The flight from the institutional framework kills every hope of reform and is, moreover, nearly always based on utopian ideas. Realism is an important ingredient of the true ecumenical attitude.

One must be ready not to avoid the suffering connected with the road to reunion, but to accept it loyally. Christ broke down the wall of division by carrying His cross till the bitter end. We should not allow ourselves to become embittered by the irritating character of certain theological positions and ways of acting that are deeply embedded through four centuries of bitter conflict. Before pronouncing any judgment, one must inwardly arrive at

13. *Ibid.*, p. 95.

willingness to take upon oneself the suffering connected with dividedness.

Thus, ecumenism demands dedication and loyalty to one's own ecclesial community. The price of this solidarity is the loyal acceptance of the defective character inherent in one's own spiritual family. Without this loyalty and the suffering it entails, any kind of ecumenism is only a cheap parody. Ecumenically speaking, then, it is difficult to excuse one's living in inner aloofness and alienation from his own religious community.

3. *Solidarity of the Protestant with Protestantism*

We are called to unite, to be men of peace with all men, and particularly with our Brothers who belong to the same confessional family. SPIRITUAL DIRECTIVES[14]

For a Protestant, solidarity with his own Church tradition means that he is united with all groups within this tradition. Taizé's rule to "love your neighbour, whatever may be his political or religious beliefs,"[15] applies in a very special and concrete way to the neighbour living within Reformational Christianity. Prior Schutz indicates the reason for this special emphasis within this particular Christianity:

According to the ideas of puritanical Protestantism it is better to have a Church numerically small, purified of the half-hearted and the well-wishers, freed from the old leaven of hypocrisy and conformity.

At the heart of Protestant thinking there is often a tendency to prefer divisions—better to separate from men who uphold tradition, the conformists who seem to embody the opposition of reaction, rather than to put up with them.[16]

14. *The Rule of Taizé* and *Spiritual Directives,* p. 105.
15. *Rule of Taizé,* p. 15.
16. *Unity Man's Tomorrow,* p. 47.

We mentioned already how Taizé has embodied in its own community solidarity with the diversity of Protestantism which is a consequence of the Reformation. The Community embraces German and Scandinavian Lutheranism, Dutch, Swiss and French Calvinism. Nevertheless, its Protestantism can be put under a single heading: it is orthodox. The Community now tries to find ways not to limit its solidarity to like-minded "right wing" Protestantism but to extend it to the Free Churches and sectarian movements. A concrete form of this solidarity is financial assistance, which is now being attempted in favor of a Pentecostal hospital in Chili. It would be easy to remain aloof from certain groups within the Reformational tradition and then to discuss, unhampered, unity with carefully selected Christians of other persuasions. "It is so easy," says Prior Schutz, "to call sectarian this Baptist, that Pentecostalist, or still another [of the 'sects'] in whom we fail to recognize ourselves. Nevertheless, their position is a consequence of the Reformation, and therefore solidarity imposes itself."[17]

4. Solidarity of the Catholic Within Catholicism

> It is important to give up the unhappy habit of putting labels on everything, of putting Christians in the categories of "progressive" or "conservative," and thereby putting them out of count without realizing that by doing so we are already destroying something of the very body of Jesus Christ. ROGER SCHUTZ[18]

A Catholic worthy of the name owes ecumenical solidarity to all his fellow Catholics. He may not exclude any group from the action radius of his esteem. A willingness

17. *Dynamique du provisoire*, p. 111. In 1965 and 1966 there were encounters in Taizé with the Salvation Army, Pentecostalists, Plymouth Brethren and Baptists.
18. *Unity Man's Tomorrow*, p. 56.

to be reconciled, even with a fellow believer, is here also a guarantee of an authentic desire for unity. It is useful to hear this truth affirmed by non-Catholics. The Council period has shown very clearly how much diversity exists within the Catholic Church, and this diversity demands a major effort of catholicity. It is wrong to demand all rights for one trend of thought and to deny genuine esteem and any sign of solidarity to those with whom we disagree among our fellow believers. It would be a serious blow to the ecumenical movement if the slogan became accepted that "progressives have no dealings with conservatives" (cf. John 4:9).

Bitterness, Prior Schutz said on the occasion of a visit paid to Taizé by a Dutch ecumenical group never works to the good of unity. The irritating aspect contained in the conduct of certain authorities of one's own Church or of another ecclesial communion, the opacity of existing canonical regulations or of their application, the diversity of interpretations which different official authorities give to prevailing laws—all this one must accept with the greatest possible spirit of fair play.

Ecumenical solidarity applies especially with respect to those who "lag behind." A crucial test of the authenticity of our unitary intentions lies perhaps in an examination of our solidarity to see whether or not it extends to those who—in our own Church or in any other—are most burdened with the weight of habit or petrified tradition. It would be easy to limit one's brotherly love to "progressives" and to turn away from fellow Christians who are "integralists" with bitterness of heart, false shame or a cold shoulder. "Do not even the gentiles do the same?" (Mt. 5:47). This matter especially will show how much effort authentic ecumenism demands. One cannot be satisfied with a "let them talk" or with tolerating them while shrugging his shoulders. Ecumenism implies an active flexibility, a loyal effort to get along with all and a solidarity that sincerely wishes to take into account those who think differently among one's fellow believers. Without sharing their standpoint, one will have to make room for them in the ecclesial community, and do it without smugness.

The same attitude must be demanded of the "conservatives" with respect to their more "progressive" fellow Christians. No matter how much they think that they are obliged in conscience to sound the alarm, they must openly, and not in underhanded fashion, fight for their standpoint and repress the inclination to see the others as wolves in sheep's clothing, anarchists, or unprincipled seducers.

In one of his works, written after he had attended three sessions of Vatican Council II, Prior Schutz wrote: "In this period of history, we expect of Catholics that they do not close themselves to one another. If the different trends that manifest themselves prevent dialogue, this would constitute an unparalleled trial for ecumenism."[19]

5. *Solidarity of Catholic Religious with Their Own Institute*

> *Be prepared at all times to forgive. . . . He who lives in mercy knows neither susceptibility nor disappointment. He gives himself simply, in self-forgetfulness.*
> RULE OF TAIZÉ[20]

By its very existence the Community of Taizé offers Catholic religious an opportunity to compare their own way of life and their communities with the suggestions of Taizé. Taizé does not at all wish to pose as a judge or as an example for others and makes every effort to avoid even the appearance of doing so. Nevertheless, it invites

19. *Dynamique du provisoire,* p. 109.
20. Pp. 43 and 46.

reflection, which is also the aim of this book. Such a
reflection does not at all imply unfaithfulness to one's
own religious institute. As a matter of fact, many Catholic religious have been re-assured about the essential viability of their vocation by the existence and the witness of
Taizé. For them, a comparison with Taizé contains an
encouragement of potential renewal. There are others,
however, whose bitter disappointment with their own religious institute increases when they compare it with the
Taizé community. It is to the latter that Prior Schutz
addressed a section of his *Letter to Religious* on the occasion of the inauguration of the Church of the Reconciliation, on August 6, 1962. Several parts of it have been
reprinted in his book, *The Dynamics of the Provisional.*

> There are a few among you who no longer wish to
> remain united with their own in the difficult course of
> their vocation. Some of these then prefer to question
> their first commitment, at the risk of rupturing the unity
> of their person. But one does not with impunity break up
> that unity.
> Others utter threats. But one does not reform a body,
> no matter how small, by threatening to break away from
> it. It is always from within and with infinite patience
> that one re-animates what ought to be re-animated. Only
> in this way is a confrontation constructive.[21]

The same idea is often repeated by Prior Schutz. For
instance, in his work *Unity Man's Tomorrow* he says:

> When people pass through a period of tension in
> married life or in any other form of Christian commu-
> nity, it is quite obvious that a separation would make for
> a momentarily relaxed atmosphere. That is why the
> breaking up of a solemn vow is able at first, because of

21. *Aujourd'hui, Journal de Taizé,* No. 1, March, 1963, p. 13.

the dislocation it brings about, to bring real relief—indeed the beginning of a kind of expansion. But some processes which take place in the deepest parts of the personality can only be assessed in the light of a long lapse of time. After a period of feeling all right, an abandoned marriage or priesthood for example can lead to a serious new crisis unless one deliberately gives up the attempt to maintain integrity and to achieve unity of the person.

It must be recognized that every separation, though for the moment it might do away with tension, is definitely an impoverishment. We therefore cannot wish any Christian, still more any Christian group, to suffer such an impoverishment.[22]

6. *Ecumenical Spirituality and the Unity of the Churches Among Themselves*

> *Never resign yourself to the scandal of the separation of Christians, all who so readily confess love for their neighbour, and yet remain divided.* RULE OF TAIZÉ[23]

The Brothers of Taizé do not wish to resign themselves to the divided condition of Christians. For two thousand years the mission of unity and reconciliation has been entrusted to the Christians, and it is this which makes their mutual division so much more absurd and abnormal. Cordial relations among divided Christian denominations are merely a first step, not the final goal. It is not inconceivable that, after the first enthusiasm of ecumenical *rapprochement* has died down, Christians would think that they have arrived where they wished to be and that they would thereafter be satisfied with a friendly co-existence. The atmosphere would be a little less tense, but the division would be maintained.

22. P. 47. The *Spiritual Directives* (p. 97) express the same thought in a slightly different way: "All rupture appears for the time being to relieve the tension, which in the long run is an impoverishment and a failure."
23. Pp. 15-16.

Christian dividedness means mutual impoverishment and, above all, it renders powerless the evangelical message to the world. The Christians claim to announce peace, reconciliation, and unity to the world; but, at the same time, they fight among themselves or at least remain aloof from one another. Visible unity, then, is a primary necessity both for the sake of the Christians themselves and for that of the world:

> The first adaptation of Christians to the modern world must be to present themselves in it in unity, lest they throw doubt on [Christian] love before they even speak of it.[24]

From the very beginning of their foundation, the Taizé Brothers sought ecumenical contacts; for example, with the apostle of unity Father Paul Couturier, with the worker-priests, with Catholic monasteries, Eastern Orthodox patriarchs, Cardinal Ottaviani, Pope Pius XII and especially Pope John XXIII, and the "Catholic" population of the village of Taizé and its surroundings. Daily the Brothers pray for the visible unity among Christians and, since the opening of The Church of the Reconciliation, more and more people pray with them for that intention. This church contains a crypt for Catholic worship and a chapel for the Eastern Orthodox. Thus, both the dividedness of Christians and their praying-together are made permanently present at Taizé.

If unity is the work of God, who creates mankind to be a unity, and of Christ, who has broken down the wall of division through his death on the cross, the Christian expectation of reunion and reconciliation will primarily be based on what God will do in Christ. It is not the conference table that is the primary factor of unity, but men's

24. Sammy Chabrillan's summary of his interview with Prior Schutz, *Panorama chrétien*, July, 1963, p. 23.

availability for God. This does not mean that we can neglect dialogue, study and publications. Taizé itself fully shares in these activities, even though the Community is convinced that no human enterprise can replace prayer for unity and for God's action toward this unity. The interhuman dialogue must be encompassed by this prayer, and the ecumenical attitude must be permeated with it. For this reason the Community's interest lies strongly in the direction of ways which lead to unity of life and of confession on the basis of man's "practice of piety"—*viz.*, the liturgy and life according to the principles of the Gospel.

When I visited Taizé during the Pentecost week of 1959, Brother Prior began a conversation by indicating a few characteristics which, in his view, should be typical of an ecumenical attitude. The first and most important of these is "to seek first of all Christ; Him above all." In Scripture, in the Eucharist, in prayer and in life itself, "Christ must live in me." The Christian ecumenical attitude of life finds its driving force in this desire to make Christ live in oneself.

This inner bond with God in Christ, the Prior added, will then reveal itself in many ways in one's external conduct. For example, an ecumenical spirituality demands that one endeavors to avoid sly and devious tactics in his relationships with Church authorities. That kind of "cleverness" does harm to unity. A "certain ingenuity supported by prudence" is better than a calculating slyness. Camouflage and ambiguity are not recommended by the Gospel, which expresses a preference for the "simplicity of the dove."

The true ecumenical attitude demands also that one take the greatest care not to provoke crisis situations or conflicts. If one foresees that his action will endanger an existing unity, he must seriously consider whether it would not be better to avoid that action. Where speaking would nourish bitterness, heighten the tension of an atmosphere that is already highly charged, or where a statement would set one section of a community against another, there it is more ecumenical not to speak, no matter how avid the audience would be or how popular the word would appear.

For this reason the Taizé Brothers never speak or act in a situation which might displease the established Church authorities, whether the latter be Catholic, Lutheran or Calvinistic. In this spirit Prior Schutz wrote in his *Letter to Religious:*

> When we are told of a certain uneasiness weighing down this or that one of your institutions, we remain silent, for it is only too true that outside judgments always produce the result of hardening the positions. . . . And if it is given to us to express ourselves, we do so only when we are certain that it will not foster a spirit of revolt.[25]

Ecumenism and reconciliation demand a kind of death to oneself. This implies especially that one renounces the idea of converting Christians of another denomination to one's own. It does not mean that one's pastoral concern should exclude Christians of a different denomination, but that one must try to help him in the Church to which he belongs so that in it he can become a leaven. Generally speaking, Christian unity is better served by bringing Christians closer to Christ in their own ecclesial tradition.[26]

25. *Aujourd'hui, Journal de Taizé,* No. 1, March, 1963, p. 13.
26. In the *Revised Report of the Commission on "Christian Witness, Proselytism and Religious Liberty,"* drafted by the Commission at St. Andrews, August, 1950, we find the following recommendation under the heading "Principles which should guide Churches in their mutual relationship": "3. That we recog-

The required death to oneself demands also that we do not rejoice over the weakness and defects of other churches. The visible unity of Christians is not served by the degradation or languor of an ecclesial body. Some Protestant evangelists in South America are delighted by the difficult situation encountered there by the Catholic Church. They react to the tension in Latin America Catholicism by hoping and wishing for a split in that Church. Such an attitude is not ecumenical at all. For the sake of the coming unity, each Christian group must be ready to sacrifice anything that is not essential. The unity of Christians will not consist in the triumph of one group over the others. As Prior Schutz says:

> [Our ecumenical work] is only of any use if we expect our brothers to make steps which they find possible— instead of asking them to make those which their faith

---

nize the right of the mature individual to change his Church allegiance if he becomes convinced that such a change of allegiance is God's will for him" (*The Ecumenical Review*, vol. 13, 1960-61, p. 88). Abstracting from what the individual change of allegiance means for the person himself, we would like to draw attention to the following point. From an ecumenical standpoint such a switch sometimes should not be characterized first and foremost as a break with the unity (of the former church) but rather as an actual contribution to the hopefully expected unity that is to come. For example, for certain Protestants who have joind the Catholic Church their change to Catholicism does not at all mean a betrayal of their Reformational faith. Without any resentment, but full of gratitude for their Reformational past, they endeavor to give new life to the authentically Christian accents of the Reformational confession and to integrate them with the Catholic tradition. True, they gave up the opportunity to become an ecumenical ferment within their former Church communion; sometimes they even saw themselves forced to do so because their ecumenical tendencies met too much opposition in their former environment. The ecumenical value of individual changes of allegiance will be less according as there is more resentment against one's own past, according as one negates this past, instead of bringing it into the new Church to which one has given his allegiance. In such a case, the change means indeed a break and is therefore unecumenical.

makes impossible; if we are ready ourselves to make those that do not contradict our fundamental convictions. It will be effective if we give up all facile ways of thinking as we prove our absolute loyalty in regard to other confessions.[27]

Catholics should keep in mind that it is insulting for their separated brothers to speak of the latter's "return" to the Church. The movement toward unity does not go back but goes forward. One who conceives unity as the liquidation of one and the preservation of the other shows a woeful lack of understanding of what Christian unity means.[28]

Protestant can fall into a similar illusion and think that the road to unity will imply that the Catholic Church take over the principles of the Reformation. But, "Does that not mean," Prior Schutz asks, "that they entertain a mentality of 'return' which is not at all different from the one they object to in others? We would merely have to remain what we are and wait for the Catholics to come to us."[29]

All Christians are in the situation of tension between a unity already given by Christ and a unity that is still to be achieved. No Christian Church can permit itself to mark time, for all of us live in a period in which the Body of Christ is built up "until we all attain to the unity of the faith and the knowledge of the Son of God, to mature manhood, to the measure of the stature of the fullness of Christ" (Eph. 4:13). All Churches still carry the pilgrim's

27. *Unity Man's Tomorrow,* p. 75.
28. For some Catholics it is difficult to rid themselves of the idea that they "have arrived" at the goal the others should reach. On hearing about Taizé and its views, they are likely to exclaim: "These Brothers are no longer far away from us. How marvellous would it be if they were to come all the way!" Let us keep in mind that all Christian congregations still carry the pilgrim's staff: all of us are still on the way.
29. *Dynamique du provisoire,* pp. 126 f.

staff and are still "on the way." Visible unity still lies ahead, it has not yet been achieved by anyone. It is not a question of some having to "find again" this unity, but of all making an earnest attempt to gain it.

As a condition for ecumenical dialogue, Brother Robert mentions also "a spirit of research." This condition implies a kind of spiritual youthfulness, a constantly renewed resistance to the sclerosis or paralysis of a premature senility. A physician, Brother Robert compares the ecumenist with the man of science: research seems to be conditioned by a certain age; thereafter, man's imagination is exhausted and he often lacks the ability to raise genuinely new questions. His activity is then limited to teaching. The Christian must as long as possible try to remain open to the "spirit of research" and not limit himself to repeat what has been commonly accepted. Brother Robert quotes Bishop Marty who, in a colloquy held at Taizé between bishops and Protestant ministers, in September, 1960, called the Holy Spirit a "perturbing Spirit," a Spirit who prevents us from comfortably settling down. And the same speaker defined the role of a bishop as that of one "who must maintain perpetual revolution in his diocese."[30]

30. *Aujourd'hui, Journal de Taizé,* No. 8, Oct., 1964, p. 2.

CHAPTER NINE

ECUMENICAL ACTIVITIES

THE PRECEDING PAGES presented a more or less orderly survey of the various aspects involved in the ecumenical spirituality promoted and lived by the Brothers of Taizé. We must now draw attention to some of the most important activities in which the Community gives expression to its ecumenical attitude.

1. Hospitality

With the growing number of visitors, we run into the danger of cutting ourselves off from them, by reclusion, in order to defend ourselves. . . . People who come to us expect bread, and if we present them with stones to look at, we shall have fallen short in our ecumenical vocation. SPIRITUAL DIRECTIVES[1]

Perhaps it was only *post factum* that the Brothers of Taizé realized the important role which their new Church of the Reconciliation, would play in their ecumemical work. This church is not a monastery building, lying inside an enclosing wall that protects but also hides it. Like the old village church itself, this new structure stands accessibly and invitingly in a free space. Since its opening on August 6, 1962, it has become evident how much

1. *The Rule of Taizé and Spiritual Directives,* pp. 99 f.

this church serves not only the Community but also the *ecumene,* the entire people of God.

The Church of the Reconciliation is built like a ship, a ship on which embarks the entire variety of the Christian world, as well as those who belong to no church or are unbelievers. It has become a place of pilgrimage in the modern style. Throughout the summer and deep into the fall, many thousands of people come to it: day or week-end tourists, neighborhood groups, Protestants guided by their minister, retreatants, students, priests, nuns, men belonging to no Church, bishops, Lutherans, Englishmen, Germans, seminarians, missionaries, participants in "work-communities." Many come simply as sight-seers to satisfy their curiosity; others have explicitly religious intentions; still others combine the two. But, as an article in Taizé's *Journal* points out, it is not mere insignificant curiosity that induces man to travel or to go on trips. His need to travel arises also from the desire to escape briefly from the grip of every-day life, from the stultifying regularity of worn-out experiences, from the over-familiar. These trips serve to raise his sensitivity to new impressions and to renew it. His power of absorption is, as it were, rejuvenated by his travels. Things and relationships which fail to draw his attention at home now strike him and have a chance to impress themselves on him.

The Brothers wondered what would be the best way to meet this invasion of visitors with their increased sensitivity to impressions. They decided to use the opportunity to let the visitors perceive a dimension of the Church that they had perhaps never before experienced. The visitor climbing up the hill of Taizé should be offered the visible sign of a praying community "from every nation, from all tribes and peoples and tongues" (Ap. 7:9) and, if possible, he should be taken up into it, into this prayer for the visible unity of all Christians, for the bond of union of all men, of which he experiences here a foretaste. In this way even the casual and unbelieving passer-by may be able perhaps to perceive that Christians are finally taking their heritage a little more seriously.[2]

Three times a day the Brothers sing their office in the church. Visitors can unobtrusively and without fear of compromising themselves join in, for there are always many people present, and they need not be afraid of being intruders in a monastic gathering that is not really meant for them. Vespers especially, and in particular on Sundays, is crowded. Some people remain standing before the open entrance of the church, so that they can feel free to leave when they wish. Usually, however, they too stay to the end, instead of merely satisfying a passing curiosity.

The office is preceded by a liturgical-pastoral introduction, attuned to the heterogeneous and unknown visitors. The Brothers have adapted themselves to the visitors in this service and substituted for their usual monastic Office a more universal form of prayer which can be assimilated by everyone. Later in the day, in their own Sunday evening compline this pastoral preoccupation makes room again for simple praise of the Lord. Commenting on the effect the Office has on those visitors, Brother Robert writes:

> For many, as experience shows, it is a kind of shock, the first beginning of a "fundamental crisis" which sets their personal faith into motion and leads to serious reflection.[3]
>
> Certain echos made it possible for us to know what a shock such an encounter with the Church can provoke in some people. In this way the liturgy and the prayer in common of Christians of different denominations assume a missionary value.[4]

2. *Aujourd'hui, Journal de Taizé*, No. 5, Jan., 1964, pp. 4 f.
3. *Aujourd'hui, Journal de Taizé*, No. 8, Oct., 1964, p. 4.
4. *Ibid.*, No. 5, Jan., 1964, p. 6.

We have recorded this matter under the heading "hospitality." The mere fact that the Community attuned its Office to the stream of visitors would suffice to justify this classification. This is not the only reason, however. One could imagine that, aside from opening liturgical assemblies to visitors and attuning the service to them, the Community would withdraw from contact. A heterogeneous stream of visitors, and especially of tourists, is sooner or later felt as an intrusion, against which one protects himself by a kind of aloofness. Taizé could have felt satisfied with its liturgical openness. Yet the Brothers thought that it would not be enough to show buildings and a liturgy to the people visiting Taizé, for among those tourists there are many men seeking answers to their questions. Those people should find also fellow human beings; they wish to see "the face of a brother rather than the severe figure of the institution."[5] One of the Community's households is charged with the reception of visitors. When the Rule of Taizé was composed, the Brothers may not have suspected that this reception would become such an important part of their ministry. Yet, they wrote: "It is Christ himself whom we receive in a guest. Let us learn to welcome; let us be willing to offer our leisure time; let hospitality be liberal and exercised with discernment."[6]

Accordingly, the Brothers do not block themselves off from the visitors. By way of the specific household charged with the guests, they come to meet them—an arrangement that permits the other households to do their work without being unduly disturbed. The Community has also initiated a continuation of the unity realized in the liturgy: after the office they invite some of the visitors to an *agape*, by sharing the Brothers' meal. "It is by partaking of

5. *Ibid.*, No. 5, Jan., 1964, p. 4.
6. *Rule of Taizé*, p. 65.

the one loaf that we, who are many, are made one Body." Although this meal is not a Eucharistic supper but an infra-sacramental communion, its importance for a future Eucharistic communion should not be underestimated. To make this Christian reception possible on a wider scale, the Brothers in 1963 began to serve a so-called "table for pilgrims" for those who had come from afar. And the accommodations for the reception of guests continue to increase.

To provide at least a minimum of attention for the many guests and visitors, the Brothers saw themselves forced to make an appeal to the aid of others. The Protestant Sisters of Grandchamp, Switzerland, effectively help them in their hospitality. These Sisters receive visitors at or near The Church of the Reconciliation and answer their questions or give them an opportunity to express their desires. Catholic Sisters of St. Charles, of St. André (Belgium) and a few Dominican Sisters from nearby Bonnay act as hostesses at the center of encounter at Cormatin and at the "center of welcome" at Taizé itself. One who as a guest has seen the work of these Sisters is inevitably filled with the greatest admiration. A special witness emanates from the way these ladies—the Sisters dress in civilian garb—receive the endless stream of new guests, especially at the "table for pilgrims." Speaking about them, Prior Schutz says: "When near a community [of men] the presence of women, supported by the hidden offering of their lives, comes to underscore a [kind of] complementarity, the welcome is made very large and ample. Without them, that would have been impossible."[7]

In addition, since the spring of 1964, there exists a fraternity of Catholic Franciscans in one of Taizé's houses. These Friars share as much as possible in the life of the Community and also take part in the reception of

7. *L'Unanimité dans le pluralisme*, Taizé, 1966, p. 48.

visitors and in answering their questions. The Catholic celebration of the Eucharist is taken care of by them in the above-mentioned crypt of the Church of the Reconciliation. There are also two Orthodox priests for the Eastern rite service in the Church's special chapel. Finally, since 1964, there is every summer a group of young laymen who render assistance with the reception of visitors. In this way Protestants, Catholics, Orthodox, religious and laymen work together as brothers. On the road toward future visible unity, inveterate prejudices can be removed only by this kind of encounter with, and discovery of fellow-men who "think differently."

Day in, day out, all kind of people pass through this modern place of "pilgrimage,"[8] to go home with impressions and resolutions known only to God. One visitor worded his impression in the following way: "In Taizé the walls separating the Churches have become as transparent as glass and they stand under heavy pressure. The Church as institution experiences here the pressure of the Church as community."[9]

Taizé is no perpetual "open house," however. It owes its identity and its profound "presence to the world" to its spiritual privacy and reserve. What the Brothers wish to offer their visitors and what they hope to receive from them in openness and sharing is closely connected with their spirit of recollectedness and interior life. Availability cannot be identified with dissipation. On the contrary, it demands a high degree of common and individual concentration. As the *Spiritual Directives* say:

> While preserving our deeper life, keeping a certain
> discernment and avoiding feverish dissipation, let us

8. In 1963 the number of visitors was estimated at 150,000. There were also 8,000 people who registered for retreats or meetings (so-called *sessionnaires*).

9. Reverend N. van den Acker, "Taizé, een impressie," *Oecumene,* vol. 4 (1965), p. 293.

remember on every occasion how to be open and hospitable. We cannot allow ourselves either cold indifference or the familiarity often desired of us by some guests who would quickly disqualify our vocation and deceive our guest's very expectations. . . . People seek in us men who radiate God. This implies a life hidden in God, so that the presence of Christ which is borne by each Brother may be renewed within us.[10]

Let us dwell briefly also on a less improvized form of hospitality which is increasingly practised by the Taizé community. Many guests remain for several days to participate in organized colloquies, congresses or retreats. There are retreats or "encounters" for mixed marriages, under the guidance of Catholic and Protestant ministers, for students, teachers, married couples, and youths. The polyglot community need not limit itself to a single language and loves to use these meetings to bring together people of different nationalities.

A group of German young men worked for sixteen months at the building of The Church of the Reconciliation. For both the Community and these young men themselves, it developed into a very special experience. Common manual labor revealed itself endowed with a great value for communication and a strong formative power for the construction of a genuine community. When it became obvious to the Brothers that additional building projects would be necessary, they decided to make use of the potentialities revealed by this form of collaboration. Since the fall of 1963 they organized so-called "work-communities" lasting two weeks during the summer and longer periods during the winter. In this way the meeting centers of Taizé and Ameugny were built, and similar work was done for the Orthodox center.

The three pillars of these work communities are prayer,

10. *The Rule of Taizé and Spiritual Directives*, pp. 99 f.

manual work and study.[11] Three times a day all those
who dwell on Taizé's hill gather for prayer in common.
Here, in common worship, is the place of true communion with the Brothers and of sharing in the essential
dimension of their life. Four hours a day are set aside for
manual labor on a construction site. This work gives all
an opportunity to encounter and discover their fellow
workers, in the communion resulting from the accom-
plishment of a task that is exacting. The manual work
acts like a melting pot, in which the work community
takes shape. The remaining half day is spent in study.
Each day a specialist gives an introductory lecture, which
is followed by common reflection in discussion, by individual reading and personal conversations.

All those who came to the "work communities" at Taizé
in 1965 were asked to live in an *aggiornamento* together
with the Community. According to the Brothers' wish, the
visit of these guests to Taizé should be an opportunity to
examine themselves, to put into question everything that
is not essential, to bring themselves up to date and, by
recovering in this way genuine availability, to commit
themselves again with renewed boldness. The ecumenical
progress which the Brothers hoped their visitors would
make together with them was to go beyond dialogue and
to arrive at true collaboration among Christians. For this
purpose they proposed concrete ecumenical commitments
for one year, in order to give support to the younger
generation's ecumenical hopes and to make them participate in providing greater human dignity for the poorest
of mankind. These commitments were not limited to
prayer but also to a precisely defined form of action. At
the end of their stay, the young men made a retreat, and

11. The description of the work communities is borrowed from
the plan for 1965, as published in *Aujourd'hui, Journal de Taizé*,
No. 9, Jan., 1965, p. 4.

in its context the Brothers proposed those concrete commitments for one year.

The numerous possibilities of contact, added to the deep impression undoubtedly made by these work communities, make them means of an ecumenical, Christian-religious formation whose significance one can hardly gauge. All these young men return to their homelands bearing the imprint of the ideal for which the Community of Taizé lives. The *Spiritual Directives* ask: "How can each [Brother] respond personally to the ecumenical vocation?" The answer to this question begins with the words: "By feeding the flame kindled for unity throughout the world." The contacts the Brothers make at Taizé provide them with a unique opportunity to feed that flame.

2. *Brothers on Mission*

> *Brothers on mission, forming small radiants of unity, are bearers of Christ simply by their presence. They do not know how, but through their simple Christian presence, God assumes and transfigures this world slow to believe.* ROGER SCHUTZ[12]

Taizé is a center of ecumenical traffic and of permanent institutionalized contacts. But the dialogue is not limited to Taizé itself. The Brothers themselves also wish to be "pilgrims of unity," and their many travels enlarge and renew contacts; they create possibilities to rise high above the limited horizon of local situations and local problems. These contacts with the world at large take the form of travel for study, series of lectures or, in a more penetrating fashion, that of temporary settlements or "fraternities."

The "tendrils" of the Taizé community reach very far.

12. *L'Unanimité*, p. 49.

Its travelling Brothers and those living at fraternities are, as it were, ecumenical probes temporarily inserted in "neuralgic points" of human misery or Christian dividedness. They serve to provide orientation to the Community's vocation and initiatives.

From the very beginning the fraternities were temporary stations. "The fraternities live under tents," warn the *Spiritual Directives*.

A fraternity is a temporary settlement of a few Brothers —usually three or four—in a particular country. The Brothers live in a rented house, furnished with a few borrowed or rented beds, chairs, etc. They try to earn their living on the spot, if possible in such a way that the work of one or two leaves the others free. In a suitable place they sing their daily office, to which others are invited to the extent that this is possible. Hospitality plays an important role in these fraternities, and the Brothers like to invite guests at their table. It cannot be easy for these Brothers to hold constantly more or less the same conversations with different visitors and unceasingly to speak about the same essential points of the evangelical and ecumenical message. Interviewers follow one another as in a regular cross examination; yet the Brothers try to speak, in addition, also to some of the unannounced guests who have prayed the office together with them in the community chapel.

Aside from the improvised or organized reception of visitors, the Brothers living at a fraternity deliver addresses, organize retreats or prayer meetings. Nevertheless, in their new and temporary surroundings, the Brothers are not primarily speakers or professional ecumenical workers, but first and foremost "silent witnesses."[13] That which is accomplished by the Brother who labors in a factory or workshop is perhaps just as influential as what his speaking fellow Brother manages to instill in his audience. Writing about the function of his presence in the world of laborers, one of the worker Brothers of Taizé says:

> The presence of a Brother in the laborers' world is essentially a *sign*. My function as a truck delivery man in a large trucking company signifies our will to live the ecumenical vocation beyond ecclesial frontiers. Such a presence must be "disinterested" and silent.[14]

Aside from the fraternities we have already enumerated previously, others have existed, for example, in New Hampshire, New Jersey, Sweden, Rome (during the Council)[15], Germany (Cologne, Bad Boll), Lebanon (Beyrut) and Holland (Amersfoort). The character and meaning of each fraternity varies, but an element common to all undoubtedly is that they are centers of common prayer open to everyone. The words written by one of the Brothers concerning the value of the Office in his fraternity probably may therefore be applied also to the others:

13. " 'What do you do as a Christian?' a perfervid evangelist asked a fellow travelller in the train? 'I bake' said the man." Pursuing this striking answer, G. MacLeod continues: "The carpenter, the fisherman, the agriculturalist—or, if you will, the miner, the ironworker and the aeroplane craftsman—are God's final revelation of His purpose in creation, in the Lord Jesus Christ, of the Carpenter's shop at Nazareth, of the fishing fleet at Galilee, and of the home at Bethany. It is the truth of that which it is the Christian mission to declare till all labour is holy and every home His Temple." *We Shall Rebuild*, new ed., Iona Community, Glascow, 1962, p. 118.

14. *Aujourd'hui, Journal de Taizé*, No. 13, Jan., 1966, p. 9.

15. For a description of the work of this fraternity, see Roger Schutz and Max Thurian, *La parole vivante au Concile*, Taizé, 1966, "Liminaire," pp. 9-17.

The element which every day anew unites and binds together a group as diverse as ours is the Office. Evening prayer is the event which renews us in the joy and hope whose bearers we have been throughout our days (1 Peter 3:15). The regularity and faithfulness to the evening Office make those moments of praise and adoration become a time of refreshment in which all our tiredness seems to vanish. For the young people who share our evenings and for ourselves this common prayer materializes, as it were, our irreversible march toward unity.[16]

Better than little stories about visits to fraternities is Prior Schutz' latest book describing the sphere and the significance of these temporary establishments:

The essential task on mission is to live the joy of prayer in common, to be fraternally open to those about us. There lies our real reason for being, and everything else flows from it. Let the Brothers on mission always remember that their lives, poor and deprived of efficient means, invigorate the community. This presence permits us to have an idea, beyond a purely intellectual knowledge, of societies which otherwise would remain impenetrable to us. . . . Hospitality, constancy in common prayer, priority of fraternal life over the ministries, exchange in depth among brothers—all this disposes men to be brothers for all. In order to activate our unanimity, it is essential for the Brothers to return periodically to Taizé.[17]

Certain fraternities in dechristianized or non-Christian surroundings functioned, in the Brothers' opinion, as a kind of intense "second novitiate"; at the same time, these fraternities gave them an opportunity to discover from an ever new perspective the originality and the appeal of the Gospel. For the key to an understanding of the Good News in its purity does not lie so much in the study of the

16. Same reference as footnote 14.
17. Schutz, *L'Unanimité*, pp. 50-52.

Bible as in solidarity, in sharing and partaking, accompanied by prayer.

Life in a fraternity constantly presents a new challenge to improvise. This power of improvisation, as a condition of ever renewed availability, is of great interest to the Community. Every chance to intensify this power and willingness to improvise is deliberately and gratefully accepted. "Through their existence in diverse social milieus . . . these Brothers bring an irreplaceable spirit to the community."[18]

A visit to a fraternity suffices to show that the Brothers do not conceive detachment from material goods in a Platonic fashion. The young Brother who has enjoyed a university education and then is put to work washing frames in a factory, driving a truck for a large industrial concern, working as a laborer in a boot polish factory, as a delivery man for a trucking company, or as a worker in a shelter for homeless men, certainly gives an eloquent testimony of the freedom recommended by the Gospel.

The Rule recommends to the Brothers always to be prepared to accept uncomfortable positions whenever that is in order and to be ready to share the lot of so many of their fellow-men who hardly have the minimum required for sustenance. To be adaptable, to fight the tendency suitably to instal oneself before undertaking any work, to make shift—these are the ways in which the Brothers can express their availability to serve.

Even if a fraternity is geographically far from Taizé, it does not become autonomous but continues to work in close communion with the Community. The lecture tours, the ecumenical and social probings, and the various contacts of the Brothers all end with reports to the Community. They are like spiritual weather forecasts from all kinds of sensitive stations in the world. In using their

18. *The Rule of Taizé and Spiritual Directives*, p. 109.

initiative, the Brothers preserve their bond with Taizé, as is recommended by their Rule:

> Everywhere and at all times, they represent the Community; the witness of everyone is involved by their attitude. They keep the Prior regularly informed of their life. Let them not engage in a new venture without having his agreement, for the Prior is responsible for consulting the Council. If Brothers on mission do not give heed to this close contact, they will quickly shatter the unity of the body.[19]

To which the *Spiritual Directives* add: "The Community would quickly disintegrate and be reduced to a few conventicles."[20]

It is a difficult formula, one that combines the spirit of initiative and freedom with a strong sense of interconnection and intense collaboration. We may call it a formula of dynamic unity. By means of their advanced posts, their "pilgrims of unity," the Taizé Brothers are able to propagate the doctrine of Christian unity and, at the same time, the Community can constantly attune itself to genuine solidarity with the world. Both hospitality and mission are forms of a "presence to the world." We must now consider a third form of ecumenical activity, *viz.*, economic solidarity with the world's poor.

3. *Economic Ecumenism*

> *It is not an exaggeration to say that one of the power lines of ecumenism passes through the world of the poor.* Roger Schutz[21]

"That they all may be one, so that the world may believe" (John 17:21). The search for unity is not di-

19. *Rule of Taizé*, pp. 61 f.
20. *Rule of Taizé* and *Spiritual Directives*, p. 110.
21. *Dynamique du provisoire*, p. 78.

rected to the well-being of the Christians themselves but to the entire family of mankind. The ecumenical movement serves the task which Christians must fulfill in the world. "Unity is not an end in itself. To be one so that the world may believe! There are two steps here: the first— for us Christians to reunite, the second—for us to unite so that we can bring God to those who do not believe."[22] This unity and reunion, however, are not limited to the religious "sector" of man's existence. This unity must be an efficient collaboration and joining together of all available forces for the purpose of making true the solidarity and love of neighbor professed by all Christians. Their unity is orientated to the union of all mankind.

"Ecumenism and solidarity with the very poor go hand in hand: without economical solidarity with the poor in the Southern hemisphere, the Christians of the Western world cannot move out of that self-consideration in which the ecumenical elan is in danger of running aground."[23] For this reason the Brothers of Taizé asked themselves the question: "Is it not far away from our home that we will discover the field of action which will permit us to extricate ourselves from our mentalities in order to find the road of reconciliation?"[24] Once again we see here how the striving for Christian unity is not a purely clerical matter, but a question of life, in all its sectors.

In 1958 there still prevailed more or less a state of "cold war" between the masses of Catholics and Protestants. If they knew anything about ecumenical contacts, they either displayed a lack of interest and understanding or they excused themselves from becoming involved in ecumenism because of their incompetence and insufficient training. It was in that general atmosphere that

22. Schutz, *Unity Man's Tomorrow*, p. 18.
23. *Aujourd'hui, Journal de Taizé*, No. 9, Jan., 1965, p. 2.
24. Schutz, *Dynamique du provisoire*, p. 85.

Oscar Cullmann, a Protestant professor at Basel and at Paris, launched an idea borrowed from the New Testament in the following terms.

In the first days of Christianity there was lack of unanimity in the Church. There were two groups composed, respectively, of pagan converts and of baptized Jews; and these two groups were often in conflict because of their different ways of life and all kinds of controversies. St. Paul did not gloss over the difficulties, but he also saw that mere discussion of the differences would be insufficient and fruitless. As a sign of the unity that, in spite of everything, existed and in order to strengthen it, he therefore organized a large collection among the Christians of one group and in favor of the poor belonging to the other group. "For you know the grace of the Lord Jesus Christ, that though he was rich, yet for your sake he became poor." This ideal was the deepest motivation, but St. Paul also added: "Under the test of this service, they will glorify God . . . by the generosity of your contribution for them and for all others" (2 Cor. 8:9 and 9:13).

Cullmann proposed that the divided Christians make such reciprocal gestures of unity. It does not require any other competence than a conscious willingness to be a Christian. The Brothers of Taizé responded to his appeal. The community of goods, they argued, accepted for the sake of the Gospel and before the Church, is not an "introverted" gesture, a gesture directed only to the Community itself. As a group of celibate and mostly young men who together earned more than they needed to live, the Community asked itself what to do with their surplus earnings. We mentioned this point previously, but have to repeat it here in connection with the ecumenical gesture made by Taizé on the occasion of the International Week of Prayer for Unity in 1963.

During Vatican Council II, the fraternity residing in Rome to pray there for the Council and to serve as the home of the two Brothers "observers," received many bishops, including those of South America. The economic and social needs of that continent made such a strong impression on the Brothers that they decided to devote all their strength in the most efficient way to the underprivileged people of South America. Their decision was not entirely disconnected from Pope John's encyclical *Pacem in terris* and his plea for aid in economic development and agricultural cooperatives.

In this way the Taizé Brothers launched "Operation Hope." Its purpose is to provide possessionless Latin American peasants with tools and training enabling them cooperatively to develop the land given by South American bishops and to become its owners. The plan is not limited to mere acts of charity but accompanied by all kinds of socio-economic studies, both at Taizé and in South America. The cooperative experience of Taizé can now be utilized on a broader scale. The cooperative method is ultimately borne by the values of fraternity and solidarity. By the formation of free human communities, society at large can gradually be transformed and developed, on the basis of the freedom and dignity due to human persons and their collaboration.

Since that International Week of Prayer for Unity of 1963, Taizé has appealed to all fellow Christians who are ecumenically minded, for the aid given by Operation Hope is doubly ecumenical. Although it is still primarily directed to the possibilities that have arisen in South America on lands ceded by the Catholic Church, it also extends to Protestant development projects in Asia, to social measures for Greek Orthodox farmers on Patmos, and to support for a social development plan of the Pentecostal movement in Chili. Operation Hope enables Christians of diverse denominations to give new actuality to St. Paul's ecumenical gesture, in the sense suggested by Oscar Cullmann.[25]

The project is ecumenical also in a second sense. The world is not only afflicted by the dividedness of Christian Churches but also by an economical split. If the Christians wish to make the Gospel intelligible to all, then they must apply the consequences of this Gospel and share their spiritual and material goods with the less fortunate parts of mankind. If only all Christians could join together to give new hope for a life worthy of man to those who have given up hope! If only they could together establish some visible signs of hope in the world of the hopeless! That is also the wish expressed by Vatican Council II's Constitution on *The Church in the Modern World*.

Operation Hope has already established such signs in a dozen places on the South American continent. In Brazil, Chili, Peru, Bolivia, Uraguay and Argentina families have been provided with dwellings, agricultural tools and training; cooperative stores have been opened and refrigeration introduced, agricultural courses have been or-

25. Cf. Vatican Council II's *Decree on Ecumenism*, Ch. 2, No. 12: "Cooperation among Christians vividly expresses that bond which already unites them, and it sets in clearer relief the features of Christ the Servant. Such cooperation, which already has begun in many countries, should be developed more and more, particularly in regions where a social and technical evolution is taking place. It should contribute to a just appreciation of the dignity of the human person, to the promotion of the blessings of peace, the application of Gospel principles to social life, and the advancement of the arts and sciences in a truly Christian spirit. It should also be intensified in the use of every possible means to relieve the afflictions of our times, such as famine and natural disasters, illiteracy and poverty, lack of housing, and the unequal distribution of wealth. Through such cooperation, all believers in Christ are able to learn easily how they can understand each other better and esteem each other more, and how the road to the unity of Christians may be made smooth." Text quoted as in *The Teachings of the Second Vatican Council*, Newman Press, 1966, pp. 195 f.

ganized, advisory offices established for cooperative undertakings, planners and other experts have been engaged.

This socio-ecumenical campaign is accompanied by another, *viz.*, the publication of an ecumenical edition of the New Testament, which will be distributed in proportion to the number of baptized persons belonging to the respective Christian denominations. The edition runs to one million copies of a new translation produced with the collaboration of Catholic and Protestant exegetes from Spain and Latin America.

Writing about these South American ventures, Prior Schutz says:

> The ecumenical vocation is a privileged place in which one learns that there is reciprocity in all things. Penetrating into Latin America, we would be unable to make a paternalistic gesture, for it is we who receive an abundance of inestimable goods. The peasants of that continent give back to us the sense of God's providence which we are losing in a secularized West. Our becoming aware of our contemporary status stimulates us to the sharing of material and spiritual goods among the Christians of the Northern and Southern hemispheres.[26]

It is by means of such a solidarity and collaboration that Christian union can regain its convincing power in the world. The preaching of the Gospel to the world will remain sterile unless it is done in and by a community of human beings who, in spite of their heterogeneity, find one another in Christ and are reconciled in Him. Must not the contemporary call for unity sound false and intolerable to people who do not belong to any Church, as long as they get the impression that unity is merely an internal Church affair discussed in a pious ghetto situated in a hungry world?

26. *Aujourd'hui, Journal de Taizé,* No. 13, Jan., 1966, p. 2.

162 AN ECUMENICAL LIGHT

Cenobitic communities used to be known as "cloistered." This term is derived from a Latin word meaning "an enclosed place." The separation or "apartheid" suggested by this term cannot be applied to Taizé, save insofar as it refers to the recollectedness and privacy required for interior and religious community life. Taizé is a community in which the tension between Church and world is lived in a very special and inspiring way. In this community the closure serves a striving for unity that does not stop with fellow Christians or with a spiritualized form of irenicism, but wants authentic solidarity and all-encompassing re-union.

PART FOUR

PRAYER AND WORSHIP

Unity of faith elaborates itself peacefully, especially through liturgical prayer. ROGER SCHUTZ[1]

1. *L'Unanimité*, p. 25.

CHAPTER TEN

PRAYER AND LITURGY

The Lord could do without our intercession and our praise. Yet it is the mystery of God, that He should require us, His co-workers, to keep on praying and never to lose heart. RULE OF TAIZÉ[1]

For the superficial visitor who makes only a short visit to Taizé, the Brothers are primarily a community of worship. The praying and singing Brothers dressed in white robes is the first impression received and also the one that remains most clearly in the visitor's memory. In the same way, those who visit any one of the fraternities retain a lasting remembrance of the common prayer, reading and singing in one of the rooms of those rented houses. For, even outside Taizé, this monastic trait is not abandoned. In spite of all work in industry and the stream of visitors, praying in common and even the singing of the Office is maintained as much as possible. On these advanced posts of Taizé, the common prayer in the established style, to which visitors and guests are invited, does not interrupt hospitality. Neither in Taizé nor in the fraternities is the praying of the Office conceived as an exercise that the Brothers are not allowed or unwilling to "inflict" on a guest. On the contrary, they conceive it as a service to be

1. P. 16.

rendered to an appreciative guest, a "communion" given to him, something shared with him as a joy and not as a "job" to be done.

The first sentence of the Rule's section that speaks about prayer mentions this joy: "Just as the disciples were gathered in the temple, rejoicing and praising Thee, so I will tell all Thy wondrous deeds, for Thou hast turned my mourning into gladness and hast girded me with joy, so that my soul may sing Thy praises and not be silent."[2] Prayer is borne by joy. That is the motive given by the Rule for prayer at set times. Not the joy of the self-satisfied man, but the recovered joy of the sinful and failing man who knows that he has been forgiven, the joy of a restored inner balance, the joy of knowing that one's own rebellion and concerns are of a merely relative weight. "In the Communion of Saints, day after day, we sing the ever renewed compassions of the Lord, and His mercy quickens our fervor."[3] And: "It is often at the bottom of the abyss that the perfection of joy is given in communion with Jesus Christ. Perfect joy . . . is wonderment continually renewed before the free giving of Him who grants an abundance of spiritual and material benefits. It is thankfulness. It is thanksgiving."[4]

The Preface of Taizé's *Office* indicates as the motive for prayer the fact that man is called to give an intelligible expression to the dependence of the world and of himself on the Creator. Everything "owes" its existence to God, in the most profound sense of the term, and it is man's conscious thanks that prayer wishes to express in words. In his prayer man proclaims this true state of affairs. The daily prayer of the office hours does not want

2. *Ibid.*, p. 17.
3. *Ibid.*, p. 37.
4. *Ibid.*, pp. 38 f.

to be anything but a form and an expression of the most profound awareness of reality, the clearest possible realism that man can ever have. Conceived in this way, the daily "cycle" of prayer is not really a monastic affair, but, as the Preface of the Taizé *Office* indicates, the priestly service of everyone who is baptized, the liturgy of every Christian.

Christian tradition has sanctioned a certain kind of "institutionalization" with respect to this most profound awareness of reality, in which man, rising above the tendency to leave everything to the vagaries of his moods, summons himself, as it were, to prayer and thanksgiving at the cardinal points of the day—morning, noon and evening—in order to focus his attention on his real relationship to the Source and Restorer of his existence. It is particularly meaningful that this hymn of praise and expression of reality take place as a common prayer. For it stands to reason that mankind, which God conceived as a community, gives thanks in common and expresses its dependence on Him in common, no matter how much man's inveterate tendency to individualism would make him forget that the prayer he is able to offer is borne by his fellow-men.

The community character of institutionalized prayer puts the individual dimension that is also present in its right place and girds it with an "ecumenical" universal bond. The common prayer constantly draws man's attention to thanksgiving and praise and, thus, protects him against slavishly following his own moods or overemphasizing his own isolated importance.

At Taizé, as well as in the fraternities, the wearing of the choir robes for prayer in common and the celebration of the Eucharist helps to underscore this communal bond within which the Brother presents himself before

God. By this white garment "the Community acknowl-
edges that it is a cenobitic family in the Church";[5] and
this white robe is, at the same time, a symbol of joy and
praise, and of consecration to God.[6]

In the Eucharistic celebrations and prayer in common
the group of Brothers affirms itself as a community gathered by God. This applies equally to the Brothers at the
fraternities and those at Taizé itself. To live together, to
work together and to eat together—all these are factors
which establish and strengthen the mutual bond. But as
"regrouped by God," as a religious community from every
nation, from all tribes and peoples and tongues, the group
realizes itself first and foremost by the bond of prayer.

When in 1838 the Oxford Tractarians first pleaded for
common prayer interwoven with the natural rhythm of
the day, they faced the following alternative: Should they
simply take over the old Roman "hours" without any
change or abbreviations, or should they adapt them?
John Henry Newman viewed the introduction of these
"hours" as an "act of re-appropriation," a taking back of
an old and long-neglected heritage. The Anglican communities showed a preference for the first of these alternative solutions of the dilemma. But what was a dilemma
for them received in Taizé a solution that left no trace of
any discussion. The Brothers freely drew upon tradition
and freely restored these common hours of prayer in an
appropriate modern form. Perhaps the price of this freedom had already been paid by the Oxford men, whose
initiative had first restored tradition's right of existence.

The *Office* of Taizé is primarily a fixed formula of
prayer, composed of texts that recur with a certain peri-
odicity. It contains psalms, distributed over four weeks;

5. Brother Laurent van Bommel, "Liturgie in der Communauté
de Taizé," *Laacher Hefte*, No. XXII, Maria Laach, 1958, p. 85.
6. Cf. *The Eucharistic* Liturgy at Taizé, with an introductory
essay by Max Thurian, London, 2nd ed., 1963, p. 7.

readings from the Old and the New Testaments; a short
form of prayer in which the appointed cantor and the
others usually sing in turn and which is meant as a text
for meditation; a litany of intercessory prayers which
leaves room for the actual events happening in the world
and the interests of those whom the Brothers will meet
during the day or have recently met; and finally three concluding prayers, one of which is fixed for that whole week,
one a free prayer, and one a special fixed prayer for the
particular day of the week.

Comparing the *Office* of Taizé with the traditional
choir Office of the Catholic Church, one notes both striking similarities and meaningful differences. The Taizé
Office is strongly *biblical,* but not biblicistic. As the Preface indicates, psalms that curse enemies or verses that
call down divine vengeance on them, as well as certain
history-telling psalms, are considered less suitable for
prayer. The singing of the Office is also less frequent and
shorter than is the custom in Catholic monasteries, because the psalter is spread over four weeks instead of only
one. Moreover, Taizé follows the "natural" order of the
day in which before, mid-way and after the day's work
there is a suitable place for recollection, recovery and
re-creation. The two main parts of the Office are morning
prayer and evening prayer which, together with the
meals, are placed at "natural" breaks in the order of the
day.

The Taizé Office leaves more room also for *variation*
because the readings taken from the Bible are spread over
a three year cycle instead of the one year allotted in the
Catholic version, and, in addition, the litany of intercessory prayers follows a formula that is different for every
day within a two weeks' cycle and varies also according to
the liturgical seasons. This variable character manifests
itself even more in the practice of free prayer. The last-

named element, *free prayer,* has entirely disappeared
from the Catholic liturgical praying of the "hours," yet it
is perhaps this element that contributes most to prevent
the praying in common from becoming more or less mechanical. The rhythm of the psalms could lull one's attention asleep, and some of the Bible readings may not
always at once "strike" the listener but, as soon as someone begins to improvise—be it a "prepared improvisation"—the spiritual concentration required for improvisation communicates itself to the entire community. All
those present listen intensely, and it would be difficult to
remain aloof from this prayer's content.

Finally, *silence,* before, during and after the Office, has
an essential significance in the structure of common
prayer. It is more than merely a waiting until prayer
begins or continues. Even the casual visitor can notice
that this silence is a matter of recollecting oneself. Modern man hardly has time for silence, his life is too much a
race, but for this reason he is also more forcefully struck
by this function of silence. This silence is not an empty
moment in which the "tension" of prayer is not yet present or momentarily broken; on the contrary, it is active,
loaded and draws him along. From this preparatory or
recollective silence a power isssues forth that puts an end
to all the little noises one can usually hear in a church or
chapel; it imposes itself and gradually spreads over the
entire congregation, drawing everyone to itself and dis-
posing them to prayer in common. Silence is a creative
factor at the service of community prayer.

The absence of opportunities to improvise, of refer-
ences to actual situations in the Church and the world,
the impatience with which the sparse moments of prescribed silence (e.g., "Let us bend our knees") are met, the
length and multiplicity of official "hours" of prayer—all
these factors often give to the Catholic praying of the

Office a mechanical dimension that can seriously jeop-
ardize the power this prayer has for building up the
Christian community of its participants. Thus it can happen that for members of Catholic orders the Office de-
generates into an inescapable duty, a de-spiritualized exercise, which they continue to perform in boredom, an
established item on the program which they carry out
joylessly; it can become a time-consuming, non-creative,
periodically returning job, a blind spot in the order of the
day, which they tolerate in soul-killing resignation or
which in its boredom undermines their spiritual zest of
life and their religious elan, to make room for emptiness
and concealed dispair. As a matter of fact, if these Catholic religious participate as guests in the Office at one of
Taizé's fraternities, they are somehow taken up by the
re-creative power that goes forth from this common
prayer.

The Brothers of Taizé are very much aware of the role
that sense perception can play for people who wish to
recollect themselves in order to praise and give thanks to
the Lord in common. Singing always has a place in their
Office, even in the fraternities. The aim is not to execute
a musical performance but to present a witness. Aesthetic
sensitivity can even become an obstacle to common
prayer. Hence the Taizé Rule specifies: "During the Office,
nothing is to be gained by being upset by the difficulty
which the Brothers may have keeping in unison."[7] On the
other hand, a genuine will to pray together embodies itself
in a certain "rhythm." "In order to remedy automatism
and sustain an inner animation, long pauses of silence
help us make the time of prayer an ever new event."[8] It

7. *Rule of Taizé*, p. 21. This remark applies not only to musical
unison but to wholehearted participation in general. Not everyone
can always do it.
8. Schutz, *L'Unanimité*, p. 74.

suffices to have been present at the Office either at Taizé
or in one of the fraternities to realize that these words are
not merely a pious phrase. Common prayer demands a
certain care and cultivation of the external form: the
contact with God must become embodied even in pho-
netics. There is no question, however, of catering to an
aesthetic super-sensitivity. On the other hand, slop-
piness is also rejected: "The surrender of ourselves to a
life hidden in Christ means neither laziness nor habit; it
can be nothing other than the participation of our whole
being in the work of God through our intelligence and our
lips." Taizé's Office does not prescribe any particular bodily posture: the Brothers' posture is, we may say, ecumenical, in the senses that they equally permit postures of
Catholic, Protestant and even Islamic origin.

In the village church of Taizé, in The Church of the
Reconciliation and in the oratories of such fraternities as
those at Coventry and Amersfoort, one can always find
the *icon* of the liturgical season. It serves as a visual
reminder of the mystery celebrated during the particular
season. Placed on the center of the liturgical table or
exposed on a lectern, the *icon* makes present to the
congregation the mystery of Pentecost or that of the Pascal event. Candle light also is deliberately used to foster
reflection and reflectivity. God has become man, and He
did not avoid created things in order to come to us. Why,
then, would we not be permitted to seek Him in the same
way, by means of human and visible realities?[10] Taizé did
not reintroduce candle light to restore a forgotten relic of
the past, to preserve a strange survivor in an era that is
bathed by an ocean of electric light. The candle really
shines in the dark village church of Taizé, throwing its
soft light on the *icon* before which it burns. Light is such

9. *Rule of Taizé*, p. 21.
10. Cf. Max Thurian, *Joie du ciel sur la terre*, Paris,
1946.

a frequent biblical symbol that the accusation of seeking startling effects would have to be addressed also to the Bible itself.

"Let us seek to perceive under signs accessible to our fleshly being something of the invisible reality of the Kingdom. But let us also take care not to multiply these signs and to keep them simple, the token of their evangelical worth," says the Rule of Taizé.[11] In this way, candles and flowers have re-entered worship at Taizé. During the Easter season the pascal candle stands in the choir. The liturgical calendar of the Community contains feasts for the Name of Jesus, the Transfiguration, the New Testament Saints,[12] All Saints and, on August 15, the Commemoration of the Virgin Mary, Mother of Our Lord. On Ash Wednesway ashes are given out in the form of a cross, and during Holy Week the Altar and the Church are stripped.

Prayer in common, daily life and private prayer belong together; they do not make each other superfluous or incongruous. Someone may think that prayer is a recurrent seeking for God, an intermezzo in a day that is in other respects spent under his own control. In that case he will have great difficulty in overcoming his shyness before God. On the contrary, "God is not the one with whom we also speak from time to time during the day; He is the one with whom we spend our entire day," writes Brother Laurent.[13] The Rule of Taizé makes the same suggestion: "The praise of Christ expressed by the liturgy is effective insofar as it continues to inform the humblest

11. Pp. 18 f.
12. Saints Andrew, Thomas, Stephen, John the Evangelist, the Holy Innocents, the Conversion of St. Paul, Saints Matthias, Marc, Philip and James, Barnabas, the Birth of St. John the Baptist, Peter and Paul, Magdalen, James, Bartholomew, the Beheading of St. John the Baptist, St. Matthew, St. Michael and all the angels, St. Luke, Simon and Jude.
13. *Art. cit.*, in footnote 5, p. 78.

tasks."[14] Prayer is meant to express a fundamental attitude; it endeavors to bring together the various dimensions of life in dependence on God, the Giver of life.

Reversely, this communal liturgy of prayer can help us gradually to penetrate to the very roots of our existence, to attune our life more to God, the one who "undertakes" all life. In this way it can also foster our personal prayer in private. The Office consists largely of biblical prayer materials, it presents us with the prayer experience of many generations. One may legitimately ask whether any other "practical school" is needed for private prayer than the one provided by the interaction of liturgical prayer and daily life. In the history of religious life meditation has been gradually disconnected from communal prayer. It can hardly be news to anyone that for many people of good will the institutionalized and autonomous form of meditation, placed somewhere on the periphery of the day, has become increasingly more difficult. The harmonious way in which Taizé incorporates meditation into the communal liturgical prayer, with its explicit reference to daily life and the major events in the world, helps to make private prayer less isolated. This form of prayer is then also more easily learned, for it can be made a further specialization of the Office prayer. Private prayer and meditation exist, of course, in Taizé, but they are not institutionalized.

Undoubtedly, even with the best and most carefully arranged praying of the Office the laws governing all things human retain their power. It will not often be an effortless outpouring of the heart, and failure, which sooner or later affects all dimensions of human life, does not bypass daily prayer. Discouragement and listlessness are not barred by the walls of a church or oratory. The Office, moreover, is a supra-personal prayer; hence it can

14. P. 19.

happen that the objective sense of the texts is out of harmony with the individual Brothers' own affective moods. Nevertheless, the "hours" as prayed at Taizé possess a power that raises the praise and thanksgiving to God above the individual moods and feelings of the moment. No matter what his mood is, the individual is invited and introduced here to a fullness of biblical prayer that is already awaiting him. Thus, it may be less difficult for him to join himself to this prayer. Commenting on these difficulties, the Rule of Taizé says:

> If your attention wanders, return to prayer as soon as you notice your distraction, without lamenting over it. If you feel your weakness while actually praying, you possess nevertheless the earnest of the victory of God.
> There will be days when the Office is a burden to you. On such occasions know how to offer your body, since your presence itself already signifies your desire, momentarily unrealizable, to praise the Lord. Believe in the presence of Christ within you even though you feel no tangible response.[15]

Taizé does not advocate the road of the least resistance, as is sometimes done by others in their despair. "The balance of our life is conditioned by our attention in worship," the *Spiritual Directives* say. Regularity is recommended, rather than an early and premature capitulation, in the hope that later one's taste and need will make him again "spontaneously" desire prayer.

"Against the danger of 'mechanization' of the Office, first of all let us struggle through the inner renewal."[16] Prior Schutz latest commentary on the Rule offers a suggestion regarding things that can gradually make prayer hollow:

15. P. 22.
16. *The Rule of Taizé and Spiritual Directives*, p. 116.

Formalism! He succumbs to it for whom the common "creation" no longer springs from Christ's love and the love of his neighbor. If it is good for us to "live" prayer together at the same hours, we do it for the love of Christ, and not by virtue of a law. . . . In the time of spiritual drought we must attach ourselves to the common involvement even more faithfully than on days when faith spontaneously brings us to prayer, remembering the answers given to us in the past and the hours filled with God's presence. The sole remedy for mere habit is precisely to continue faithfully with the decision once made, and, by doing so, to be able, one day, to find again fervor.

Thus, in the hours of weariness, let us recall our former commitment, although lamenting as we accomplish it without either love or joy; and if it were to become entirely impossible to live it any longer, then it remains to abandon ourselves to Christ, in the deserts inhabited by the silence of God.[17]

Both the Rule and regularity function to safeguard the possibilities of a re-creating contact with God against the tyranny of short-sighted moods. By faithfulness to the daily Office, the Brothers hope to keep themselves in God's presence, even on days when the individual suffers from religious myopia or God remains hidden in darkness.

They believe, moreover, in the primary role of Christ: "Believe in the presence of Christ within you even though you feel no tangible response."[18] Prayer is a dialogue, but not between two partners of equal rank and equal limitation who are dependent on each other. Prayer is a dialogue of the creature with his Lord and Giver of life. The efficacy and fruitfulness of prayer is far more proportioned to His benevolence and mercy than to the vagaries

17. Schutz, *L'Unanimité*, pp. 80 f.
18. *Rule of Taizé*, p. 22.

of man's moods and of crises over which he has hardly any control. Thus, the powerless gesture of mere bodily presence itself constitutes an appeal to God's graceful benevolence. We may add that all sacramental life is such a gesture: we make helpless signs toward the liberal Source of life.

Faithfulness to prayer in common, then, is a gesture of belief toward a divine goodness that has greater value than our efforts, it is a motion of confidence in the way He will come far out to meet us, a confession of hope in the grace with which He will anticipate our powerless endeavors. The attempt to make one's regularity in prayer commensurate with one's sensitivity or moods would seem to ascribe to prayer a function at the service of spiritual self-satisfaction rather than that of placing oneself in one's need before Him who "undertakes" and is the Ground of all life. To make one's personal moods the criterion of participating or not participating in common prayer would play havoc with the idea of community; it would undermine one of the most binding elements of the religious community and end by reducing the latter to a kind of club.

To exist one must constantly return to the Source, again and again present himself before God and draw his attention to God. This presenting of ourselves together before God in expectation, Prior Schutz says, constitutes the most essential element of Taizé's community life.[19] Over the years an even more concentrated form of prayer has gradually developed in the Community:

> From year to year, without our knowing how, the call to contemplative life becomes more and more insistent—to such an extent that we were obliged to erect

19. *Fêtes et Saisons*, Jan., 1965, p. 13.

little hermitages in order to allow [community members] to withdraw there or to use them for nocturnal prayer, over and above the praying of the Office which we do together on certain nights. Some indeed experience that call to get up in order to pray, to interrupt the rhythm of sleep in order to await the arrival of Him who comes.[20]

20. *Ibid.*, interview with the Prior, p. 27.

CHAPTER ELEVEN

THE EUCHARIST

Christ, the Word made flesh, gives himself visibly to us in the Sacrament. Therefore nourish yourself with the meal of thanksgiving, the Holy Communion, and do not forget that it is offered to the sick of the People of God. It is there for you who are always weak and infirm.
RULE OF TAIZÉ[1]

For the Anglican communities, which began to arise in the first half of the nineteenth century, a feeling for the liturgy and the Sacrament had also been an effective and constructive factor. At that time sacramental life had greatly diminished in the Church of England. But the religious communities, animated by the leaders of the Oxford Movement, allowed it to develop again. On the occasion of a contact which the adviser of one of the first Anglican sisterhoods had with French Catholic religious, he was told that it was impossible to restore religious community life where there existed no vigorous sacramental practice. In other words, his interlocutors left him little hope with respect to the possible restoration of religious community life in the Church of England. The Oxford leaders themselves, however, were convinced already of the value which the incarnational and sacramen-

1. P. 20.

tal principle possesses for Christian life. In the small communities of available Christians, constituted by the sisterhoods, they brought about the realization of their sacramental renaissance.

In Taizé, likewise, this sacramental development started at the very beginning of the Community. For its members themselves this development must have been a surprising experience that was uprooting and, at the same time, enriching. In most Calvinistic Churches, the Eucharist was only rarely celebrated, and the other sacraments, such as penance, the anointing of the sick and confirmation are hardly anywhere common in the Reformational Churches. For most of the Brothers, then, their entrance in Taizé must have been the beginning of a personal evolution in a sacramental direction. For the frequency with which the Eucharist is celebrated—every day—as well the way of celebrating it differ from what one can observe in the average Protestant group.

The Brothers are free to participate in this daily celebration of the Eucharist. The *Spiritual Directives* simply say:

> In regard to frequent communion, let us remember the two examples, one of the centurion (Lord do not come into my house) and the other of Zaccheus (Lord come into my house), quoted by Saint Augustine: "For the one, it is through respect that he does not presume to receive Christ daily (I am not worthy for thee to come under my roof), and for the other, it is also through respect that he does not presume to abstain from receiving Him, even for a day."[2]

Perhaps we may say that the celebration of the Eucharist at Taizé has been the most important factor for the

2. *Rule of Taizé and Spiritual Directives,* pp. 118-119. Cf. *L'-Unanimité,* p. 75.

ecumenical inspiration of the Brothers; it may have en-
abled them, without giving up their Christian solidarity
with their own Churches, to detach themselves from a
sterile and static "marking time" deprived of any genuine
progress. One can read ecumenical works and meet with
Christians of other denominations, without any real
change in the particular denominational positions. But a
careful ecumenical—and that means here, really Christian—celebration of the Sacrament of unity and communion sooner or later is bound to dislodge the unchris-
tian lethargy which considers dividedness and separation
the normal state of affairs. Taizé's frequent celebration of
the Eucharist has perhaps made the major contribution
to the renewal that affects its expression of the faith over
the entire realm of theology. It is a renewal which, at the
same time, becomes more and more deeply rooted in the
universal Christian tradition. For the Eucharist is not
only the Sacrament of "fraternization," but also roots the
communicant more deeply in the Body of Christ, the
"dwelling" in which God gathers all together into the
"communion of saints." Thus, this Eucharistic celebration leads, as it were, spontaneously to intercommunion.

It may be useful, however, first to say something here
about the way in which the Taizé Brothers celebrate the
Eucharist. This celebration is based both on the universal
priesthood of all the faithful and on the special function
of the ordained minister.

For Catholics, the idea of the universal priesthood may
still be something they are not accustomed to. But it is
not only biblical but has also been placed again in the
center of attention by Vatican Council II.[3] The general
priesthood of the faithful is the basis for the active participation of the entire congregation in the liturgical cele-

3. *Constitution on the Church*, nos. 31, 34; *Decree on the
Ministry and Life of Priests*, no. 2.

bration. In other words, it is not a matter "of having one ordained celebrant who alone is able to celebrate the liturgy, while the rest join in to some extent with canticles or responses.[4] The presence and participation of the ecclesial community is equally indispensable for a genuinely sacramental celebration of the Eucharist because the latter is "a matter of corporate celebration."[5]

It stands to reason that in a religious community, which wishes to be an "intensely" ecclesial, the presence and participation of the members is a matter of "to be or not to be" with respect to the communal celebration of the Eucharist. As long as this celebration is looked upon as the concern of a solitary celebrant whose progress is merely being watched by the individual members of the community, the matter of everyone's presence is not really relevant. It then becomes a question of individual choice, for the Eucharist is not looked upon as a community affair but as something that will be celebrated anyhow, whether or not the individuals are present. Personal taste, periodic sensitivity and religious "need" decide, for each individual, whether or not he will be present at a service for which he bears no responsibility. In this view, the presence of community members functions merely as an added element which overcompletes a celebrant's performance that is complete in itself.[6]

4. *The Eucharistic Liturgy of Taizé*, p. 2.
5. *Ibid.*, p. 2.
6. The celebration of the Eucharist will remain ill-shaped and difficult to assimilate as long as the community's activity in it is limited to the recitation of certain prescribed formulas, as long as no appeal is made to the entire community's full human creativity, or as long as this community, in the spirit of unwitting individualism, refuses to listen to such an appeal. How often, we wonder, has not the frequent celebration of the Eucharist, through the absence of an "available" and creatively participating community, been reduced to an anemic, soul-killing, immutable and prescribed "exercise," an endless repetition of an obligatory spectacle, a half hour of passivity and mere watching! These are

The universal priesthood of the faithful that should find expression in the celebration of the Eucharist does not at all compete with the function exercised by the special office of the celebrant. His service, his *diakonia* to the community is to act as minister of Christ, to be a sign and an instrument of Christ. For the liturgy is not only a movement from below upwards, but also, and even primarily, a movement from above downwards.[7] For this reason the Taizé Brothers celebrate the Eucharist with due consideration for both the universal priesthood of the faithful and the special *diakonia* of the celebrant, who is always an ordained minister.

The order followed at Taizé in the celebration of the Eucharist is largely in agreement with traditional Western liturgy. A Catholic will find in it all elements familiar to him from the Roman missal. Nevertheless, the principle of the entire community's active participation, of the universal priesthood of all believers, has led to a few slight modifications that are suggestive and worth mentioning. It is the Prior, the "center of unity," who presides over the liturgy. This does not mean that he is always the celebrant, but it does mean that after the *Confiteor*—the confession of guilt to God and to the community—he gives the absolution; it is also the Prior who blesses the reader of the Gospel and who closes the ceremony with his blessing. The Canon of the Roman Mass is also present in the Eucharist of Taizé. The parts of it that are intercessory prayers for certain groups[8] have all been placed before the words in which the institution of the Eucharist by Christ are expressed. In Taizé, these prayers have the form of a dialogue with the congregation,

---

not purely "psychological" considerations which would leave the "essence" of the Eucharistic celebration untouched.

7. *The Eucharistic Liturgy of Taizé,* p. 4.

8. The *Te igitur,* the two *Memento's,* the *Communicantes* and the *Nobis quoque peccatoribus.*

and the people respond to them: "Lord, hear our prayer."

Singing also occupies a place in the celebration of the Eucharist, but it is restored to a genuine dialogue or responsory, even where in the Gregorian Mass it had developed into the monologue of a trained choir. For example, between the readings from Scripture, the antiphon of the *Tractus* or *Graduale* is started by the cantor but then taken up by the whole congregation. Then the cantor alone sings a verse of the psalm, and the congregation repeats the antiphon. In this way, without any elaborate rehearsals, all, even casual visitors, can participate.

The Gospel is not read in the space reserved for the Community's choir, but in a procession with candles the Gospel book is carried to the center of the church, in the midst of the congregation, for it is there that God's word must be proclaimed. Whenever there are notable groups of foreigners in the congregation, the reading of the Gospel in French is followed by that in their language. After the reading of the Gospel, the book is solemnly carried to the entrance of the church and placed on a stand near the door. Thus, on leaving, everyone is reminded to put the word into practice. These and other features make the celebration of the Eucharist at Taizé a liturgy in which the entire church is spatially, psychologically and really involved.

The Taizé Brothers practice intercommunion among themselves. Catholics who are used to think primarily, and sometimes exclusively, in terms of "validity," often ask: "Can Calvinists and Lutherans indiscriminately consecrate and receive the Lord's Supper without a unified understanding of this rite?" Max Thurian has devoted a finely nuanced article to this question of ecumenical intercommunion,[9] in which he objectively presents the

9. "Intercommunion," *Verbum Caro,* No. 66, 1963, pp. 199-213.

conditions which various Churches require for intercommunion. The condition demanded by the Lutheran Churches is "unity of faith in the real presence"; in other words, they demand a doctrinal consensus. The Calvinistic Churches start from the standpoint that Christ is the host; in principle, therefore, anyone baptized can participate. Max Thurian duly notes that among Calvinists there is sometimes a tendency to take an easy view of Church discipline regarding the Eucharist: occasionally the celebration is entrusted to laymen, women are permitted to assume the ministerial function, and there is carelessness with respect to the species left over after the celebration. Ecumenical respect at least for the other Churches would demand greater prudence in these matters. The Taizé Community strictly observes the demands of both the Lutheran and the Calvinistic standpoints with respect to intercommunion, not because of mere opportunism but as a matter of faith.

There are other conditions for intercommunion, however, conditions that could easily escape someone who thinks primarily in juridical terms of validity. "If you are offering your gift at the altar, and there remember that your brother has something against you, leave your gift there before the altar and go first to be reconciled with your brother, and then come and offer your gift" (Mt. 5:23). Intercommunion, even among members of the same Church, "when the one loaf corresponds with no spiritual reality is indeed to invoke judgement upon ourselves, by receiving the very thing our lives deny."[10] Intercommunion in life and works is the most profound condition for cultic intercommunion. Show cases along a side aisle in The Church of the Reconciliation contain photographs and statistics which offer a modern commentary

10. J. A. T. Robinson, *On Being the Church in the World,* 2nd impr., London, 1961, p. 105.

on the above-quoted text of St. Matthew: they point to the wretchedness and hunger in the world. They are an eloquent Christian reminder of what the followers of Christ must still do, and this reminder is given to them just before they are going to liturgically celebrate Christian communicative unity. This reminder is addressed to the visitors; the Brothers themselves live in a community which itself is totally an attempt to "discern" the Body of Christ (1 Cor. 11:29), that is, the Christian community.

A Catholic who is inclined quickly to resort to the criterion of validity as the only crucial and all-important issue would do well to keep this in mind. Now that practically all Christian Churches sincerely wish to enter the road to unity, intercommunion (*communicatio in sacris*) is the obligatory term of their endeavors; and with respect to this term, the question of how far one can, or unfortunately cannot yet, go is of secondary importance. We have reached the stage where it is recommended to separated brethren to pray together and to read the Scriptures together. It would not do to claim that this is "nothing," that nothing "happens" in these common services of the Word and that *therefore* they are permissible or even recommendable. The Word is sacramental and may not be opposed in such a radical fashion to the Sacrament in the stricter sense of the term. A common service of the Word is a first step toward celebrating together the Sacrament.

The intention of reserving full intercommunion for the day when the Churches reach perfect unity and recognize one another fully as the Church of Christ loses sight of the fact that the Churches, including the Catholic Church, are "on the way," are "pilgrim Churches," characterized in every respect by "provisionality." This assertion applies in particular to institutional structures, Church order and legal recognition ("validity"). The dogmatic

Constitution on the Church of Vatican Council II quite correctly devotes an illuminating chapter to this "eschatological" character of the Pilgrim Church (Ch. 7). It will be the task of theologians to explore the consequences of this character, especially with respect to the practical and inter-Church aspect.

To prevent misunderstandings, let us emphasize that there is no question of abandoning all principles when one recognizes that Church order has only a relative, not an absolute, value. Intercommunion born from indifferentism or a fading loyalty to one's own Church flatly contradicts the Christian idea of "communion." Such an attitude would make one commune with no one and nothing; no wonder, then, that one feels so "free." The common celebration of the ecumenical Sacrament *par excellence*, however, should have, neither for the individual participant nor for any participating group, the character of an antithesis with respect to his own ecclesial allegiance. There should be a dialectic between, on the one hand, loyalty to one's own visible and limited Church and, on the other, an authentic awareness of the latter's provisional character as well as a constant willingness to foster adaptation and enlargement. Such a dialectic constitutes the best guarantee for an authentic membership in the Church.[11]

Accordingly, there can be a number of reasons why at present intercommunion between Catholics and Protestants is not yet possible. Taizé does not lightly dismiss this dividedness. The Franciscan fraternity there shares the life of the Brothers, but has its own Eucharistic service. For Catholic visitors at Taizé a separate crypt in The Church of the Reconciliation is reserved for their Eucha-

11. Cf. F. J. van Beeck, "Toward an Ecumenical Understanding of the Sacraments," *Journal of Ecumenical Studies*, vol. 3 (1966), pp. 57-112.

ristic celebrations, and for the Orthodox there is a beautiful Orthodox chapel attached to the Church.

Nevertheless, there is no reason not to rejoice over the fact that Protestant Christians of different denominations are already able to practice intercommunion. The lack of esteem which some Catholics occasionally express with respect to that intercommunion must be explained through their mistaken notion regarding the value of the Sacrament in Protestant Churches. A too rigidly legalistic approach that can think only in terms of validity— "recognized" by the competent ruling authorities—makes itself felt here. To the extent that Catholics, following the prudent directions of Vatican Council II, can increasingly recognize the Protestant groups as Churches, they will experience less difficulty in acknowledging also the fruitfulness of the Protestant sacramental *praxis* and of their ministry. Thus, the day may not be too far off, we hope, that this fruitfulness will receive also official Catholic recognition in the ecclesial order, so that then the term "validity" may be dropped.

We may close this chapter with an appropriate quotation from Max Thurian:

> Separated Christians can have no greater desire for unity than that of being reunited one day in one and the same eucharistic faith at one and the same eucharistic communion, which will be the sign that their visible unity has been fully accomplished.[12]

12. *The Eucharistic Liturgy of Taizé*, p. 27.

CONCLUSION

Without the benefit of publicity, various new initiatives are born in different places of the Christian world, and experiments are made with new forms of Christian religious community life. A religious belonging to one of the "established" societies can only have the greatest respect for these experiments, and it would be good for him to take a good look at himself and his society to the fullest extent in the mirror presented by those initiatives. A girl who, instead of finishing her university studies, joins a few other young people to go and live together with two dozen psychically disturbed fellow-men addresses a wordless question to the "established" religious who happens to cross her path. To make true in this way the all-encompassing and unlimited character of the Christian idea of community, for people who are outcasts even in a Christian society but are so much in need of friends— that is an impressive way of evangelically living a common life, even if no convent bell rings, no Office is said and there is no provision for a separate liturgical service.[1]

The most important contribution made by Taizé perhaps does not so much consist in the new things it brings as in the inspiration through which the Community gives new life to old values. This witness of Taizé is particularly welcome. A vocation never fits man like a glove, for God's call repeatedly runs across man's own plans and projects. God does not call us to the plan we have devised for ourselves; His orientation of our life often takes a direction different from our own preference. Thus, it can be very helpful for us to receive encouragement to con-

1. Richmond Fellowship, founded in 1959 at Richmond, Surrey, England.

tinue on the way some of us have recognized to be God's way. In Taizé, they receive, from quarters that are above suspicion, an encouraging testimony to the value and viability of evangelical life in community.

When we show a foreigner around in our city, we are particularly eager to hear his impressions. We are also curious to hear from him what foreign papers and books say about our country. In this way we express our implicit hope of discovering a new truth about ourselves, a truth that we would not find alone. Chesterton in one of his works tells the story of a man who, instead of entering his house through the front door, broke in through the window and then again descended into it through the chimney—all this in order to get the experience a stranger would have and, thus, joyfully to remind himself that this is his own house in which he lives. The same idea also underlies a passage in his book *Orthodoxy:*

> I have often had a fancy for writing a romance about an English yachtsman who slightly miscalculated his course and discovered England under the impression that it was a new island in the South Seas. . . . His mistake was really a most enviable mistake; and he knew it, if he was the man I take him for. What could be more delightful than to have in the same few minutes all the fascinating terrors of going abroad combined with all the humane security of coming home again? . . . How can we contrive to be at once astonished at the world and yet at home in it? . . . How can this world give us at once the fascination of a strange town and the comfort and honour of being our own town?[2]

Christians are not foreigners to one another, they are not strangers and do not live in different countries. In one way or another, Taizé has given Catholic religious the chance and the joy to see anew and to appreciate aspects of their own community life that had sometimes become dull and lackluster. In addition, Taizé has given Christians a form of solidarity that did not exist before. A new part of the Gospel has been freed and, around it, we Protestants and Catholics can find one another again in unity.

BIBLIOGRAPHY

A. *Official Publications of the Community of Taizé*

The Rule of Taizé, French and English text, Packard Manse, Stoughton, Mass., 1961.

The Rule of Taizé and Spiritual Directives Following the Rule, Les Presses de Taizé, 1965.

Office de Taizé, 3rd ed., Les Presses de Taizé, 1964.

The Eucharistic Liturgy of Taizé, with an introductory essay by Max Thurian, 2nd ed., Faith Press, London, 1963.

Liturgies pascales, Les Presses de Taizé, 1962.

Aujourd'hui, Journal de Taizé, a quarterly published by Les Presses de Taizé.

B. *Publications About the Religious Life by Brothers of Taizé*

Laurent van Bommel, "Liturgie in der Communauté de Taizé. Ein Kommentar zur zweiten Kapitel ihrer Regel," *Mönchisches Leben und liturgischer Dienst*. Laacher Hefte, Heft XXII, Maria Laach, 1958, pp. 77-95.

Pierre-Yves Eméry, "L'engagement cénobitique: forme particulière et concrète de disponibilité," *Verbum Caro*, vol. 10(1956), pp. 133-160.

"La Communauté de Taizé et la passion de l'unité," *Le mystère de l'unité*, vol. 1, *Découverte de l'oecuménisme*, Desclée de Brouwer, Paris, 1961, pp. 228-238. A collective work.

"Le voeu, sacrifice d'action de grace," *Verbum Caro*, vol. 17(1963), pp. 443-472.

La méditation de l'Ecriture, Les Presses de Taizé, 1961.

Roger Schutz *Introduction à la vie communautaire*. Collection Communauté de Cluny, Geneva, 1944.

"Naissance de communautés dans les églises de la Réforme," *Verbum Caro*, vol. 9(1955), pp. 14-28.

"Résultats théologiques et spirituels des rencontres oecuméniques avec les Catholiques romains," *ibid.*, vol. 10(1956), pp. 16-22.

Vivre l'aujourd'hui de Dieu, Les Presses de Taizé, 1959. English ed., *Living Today for God*, Helicon, 1962.

"Pour un bon oecuménisme," *Verbum Caro*, vol. 11(1957), pp. 3-8.

L'unité, espérance de vie, Les Presses de Taizé, 1962. English ed., *Unity Man's Tomorrow*, Herder and Herder, 1962.

Dynamique du provisoire, Les Presses de Taizé, 1965.

L'Unanimité dans le pluralisme, Les Presses de Taizé, 1966.[1]

and Max Thurian, *La parole vivante au Concile. Texte et commentaire de la Constitution sur la révélation*, Les Presses de Taizé, 1966.

Max Thurian, "La Communauté de Cluny," *Verbum Caro*, vol. 2(1948), pp. 108-124.

Mariage et célibat, Delachaux et Niestlé, Paris, 1955. English ed., *Marriage and Celibacy*, S.C.M. Press, London, 1959.

La souffrance dans le plan de Dieu, Les Presses de Taizé, 1958.

L'homme moderne et la vie spirituelle, Ed. de l'Epi, Paris, 1961. English ed., *Modern Man and Spiritual Life*, Association Press, New York, 1964.

"Conversion spirituelle et prière pour l'unité," *Verbum Caro*, vol. 15(1961), pp. 265-283.

"Die Communauté de Taizé," *Frei für Gott und die Menschen*, ed. by Lydia Präger, Stuttgart, 1959, pp. 127-139. Originally published in *Jungenwacht*, Heft 7/8, 1957.

Introduction à la retraite spirituelle, Les Presses de Taizé, 1959.

Anonymous, "Une communauté d'intellectuels protestants," *La Vie protestante*, Nov. 6, 1942 (Geneva).

C. *Publications About Taizé by Others* (in chronological order)

Maurice Villain, "La Communauté protestante de Cluny," *Irenikon*, vol. 19(1946), pp. 153-167.

F. Boerwinkel, "De communauté de Taizé-les-Cluny," *Kerk en Eredienst*, vol. 5 (1950), pp. 346-357.

"Taizé een gelijkenis," *Wending*, vol. 8(1953), pp. 39-47.

---

1. "Together with the Rule of Taizé, this book, of which a fragment is read every day in the Community, expresses the main lines of our vocation. . . . As a commentary on the Rule of Taizé, it replaces the Customary which has never been written" (exergue on the concluding page of this book, p. 134).

F. Biot, O.P., "La renaissance de communautés 'cénobitiques' dans le protestantisme contemporain," *Istina,* vol. 3(1956), pp. 287-304.

R. Beaupère, O.P., "Vie communautaire dans le protestantisme," *ibid.,* vol. 3(1956), pp. 304-321.

Maurice Villain, *L'Abbé Paul Couturier, apôtre de l'unité chrétienne,* 1956, 3rd ed., Paris, 1959. About Taizé see pp. 177-185.

J. H. van Beusekom, *Het experiment der gemeenschap. Een onderzoek naar de plaats en de funktie van de "orde" in de reformatorische kerken,* Voorhoeve, The Hague, 1958. Summary in English.

"Le message de Taizé," *Irenikon,* vol. 32(1959), pp. 358 ff.

Robert Rouquette, S. J., "La liturgie eucharistique dans le protestantisme français et l'anglicanisme," *Etudes,* vol. 304(1960), pp. 110-115.

S. B. Marrow, "A Calvinist Cluny," *America,* vol. 102, Jan. 9, 1960, pp. 418-420.

"Further Notes on a Protestant Community," *ibid.,* vol. 103, May 7, 1960, pp. 218-219.

F. Biot, O.P., *Communautés protestantes. La renaissance de la vie regulière dans le protestantisme continental,* Ed. Fleurus, Paris, 1961.

L. H. Parias, "Que se passe-t-il à Taizé?" *La France Catholique,* Jan. 13, 1961.

"A Taizé, le frère prieur m'a dit . . . ," *ibid.,* Jan. 20. 1961.

Jean Guitton, "De Cluny à Taizé. Sur le sentier de l'unité," *Le Figaro,* Jan. 21, 1961, p. 7.

Henry Fesquet, "La communauté protestante de Taizé," *Le Monde,* Feb. 11, 1959, p. 6.

Josef Lescrauwaet, M.S.C., *Communauteit van Taizé. Parabel der christelijke eenheid,* Geert Groote Genootschap, 's-Hertogenbosch, 1961.

Charles Boyer, S.J., "Taizé, a Center of Ecumenism," *Unitas,* vol. 13(1961), pp. 239-246.

"French Protestant Monks Set an Ecumenical Example," *Jubilee,* vol. 8(1961), pp. 20-24.

Charles-Eugene Magnin, "De gemeenschap van Taizé," *Ruimte,* vol. 17(1962), pp. 41-50.

"The Eucharistic Liturgy of Taizé," *Life of the Spirit,* vol. 17(1962), pp. 45 ff.

E. Malatesta, "Taizé: an Ecumenical Milestone," *America,* vol. 107(1962), Oct. 6, pp. 840-841.

T. O'Meara, "A Liturgy of Taizé," *Worship,* vol. 36(1962), pp. 638-645.

C. F. O'Shea, "The Community of Taizé, *At-one-ment,* vol. 4(1962), pp. 146-149.

Olive Wyon, *Living Springs. New Religious Movements in Western Europe,* S.C.M. Press, London, 1963.

J. Heyke, C.S.Sp., "Het gemeenschapsleven volgens de evangelische raden in de zienswijze van de Broeders van Taizé," *Tijdschrift voor geestelijk leven,* vol. 19(1963), pp. 459-489.

T. Donnelly, "A Sign of Reconciliation," *The Furrow,* vol. 14(1963), pp. 173-179.

T. O'Meara, "The Rule of Taizé," *Review for Religious,* vol. 22(1963), pp. 318-326.

Sammy Chabrillan, "Le mystère de Taizé," *Panorama chrétien,* July, 1963, pp. 18-23.

G. Heinz-Mohr and H. E. Bahr, *Brüder der Welt,* Herder, Freiburg i.Br., 1965. With 96 photographs by Toni Schneiders.

H. N. Bonnet and J. Mignon, "Taizé, 25 ans d'oecuménisme," *Fêtes et saisons,* vol. 191, Jan. 1965, pp. 1-28.

Jean Toulat, "Per il venticinquesimo della fondazione di Taizé," *L'Osservatore della Domenica,* July 25, 1965.

Daniel Rops, "I venticinque anni di Taizé," *Osservatore Romano,* August 20, 1965, p. 3.

J. Heyke, C.S.Sp., "Oecumenisme en economische solidariteit. Het Protestant klooster van Taizé en de eenheid," *School en Godsdienst,* vol. 20(1966), pp. 13-27.

E. Henau, "Vijfentwintig jaar Taizé," *Tijdschrift voor geestelijk leven,* vol. 22(1966), pp. 31-48.

D. *Selected Theological and Liturgical Studies by Members of the Community of Taizé*

Michel Bergman, "Structures de l'Eglise pour aujourd'hui," *Verbum Caro,* vol. 17(1963), pp. 39-50.

Pierre-Yves Eméry, "Réforme et unité," *ibid.,* vol. 16(1962), pp. 42-65.

Le Christ notre recompense. Grace de Dieu et responsabilité de l'homme, Collection de Taizé, Delachaux et Niestlé, Paris, 1963.

"La Cène: une liturgie ou un sacrement?" *Verbum Caro,* vol. 18(1964), pp. 93-107.

"L'unité des croyants au ciel et sur la terre. La communion des saints et son expression dans la prière de l'Eglise," *ibid.,* vol. 16(1962), pp. 3-240.

"Les psaumes et l'unité de l'Eglise selon Saint Augustin. 'Habiter en frères tous ensemble,'" *ibid.,* vol. 19(1965), pp. 57-68.

Le sacrifice eucharistique selon les théologiens réformés français du XVIIe siècle, Delachaux et Niestlé, Paris, 1959.

Pierre Etienne, "Comme le Père m'a envoyé, moi aussi je vous envoie," *Verbum Caro,* vol. 15(1961), pp. 129-131.

Roger Schutz, "Le baptême: Appartenance fondamentale à l'Eglise," *ibid.,* vol. 19(1965), pp. 57-68.

Max Thurian, *Joie du ciel sur la terre,* Delachaux et Niestlé, Paris, 1946.

"Position de l'oecuménisme," *Catholicité,* juillet, 1947, pp. 25-26.

"Développement du dogme et Tradition selon le catholicisme moyen et la théologie réformée," *Verbum Caro,* vol. 1(1947), pp. 368-394.

"Les grandes orientations actuelles de la spiritualité protestante," *Irenikon,* vol. 22(1949), pp. 368-394.

"Jésus Christ vrai Dieu et vrai homme. Le Concile de Chalcedoine et l'unité de l'Eglise," *ibid.,* vol. 6(1952), pp. 49-58.

"L'Abbé Couturier," *ibid.*, vol. 6(1952), pp. 161-164.

"Le Saint Siège et le mouvement oecuménique," *ibid.*, vol. 6(1952), pp. 164-168.

"L'anthropologie réformée," *ibid.*, vol. 25(1952), pp. 20-52.

La confession. Collection de Taizé, Delachaux et Niestlé, Paris, 1953. English ed., *Confession,* S.C.M. Press, London, 1959.

La confirmation, consécration des laiques, Delachaux et Niestlé, Paris, 1957. English ed., *Consecration of the Layman. New Approaches to the Sacrament of Confirmation,* Helicon, 1963.

"La célebration de la nuit pascale," *Verbum Caro,* vol. 11(1957), pp. 127-153.

"Situation du sacerdoce universel et du ministère pastoral," *ibid.,* vol., 11(1957), pp. 262-268.

"Le ministère de la guérison," *ibid.,* vol. 12(1958), pp. 83-86.

"Le mémorial des saints. Essai de compréhension évangélique d'un aspect de la pieté catholique," *ibid.,* vol. 13(1959).

L'Eucharistie, mémorial du Seigneur. Collection de Taizé, Delachaux et Niestlé, Paris, 1959. English ed., *The Eucharistic Memorial,* 2 vols., John Knox Press, Richmond, Va.

L'unité visible des chrétiens et la tradition, Delachaux et Niestlé, Paris, 1961. English ed., *Visible Unity and Tradition,* Helicon, 1962.

"Unity of the Ministry," *Church Quarterly Review,* vol. 162(1961), pp. 313-334.

"L'ordination des pasteurs," *Verbum Caro,* vol. 15(1961), pp. 199-213.

"Après New-Dehli," *ibid.,* vol. 16(1962), pp. 1-7.

Marie, Mère du Seigneur, figure de l'Eglise, Les Presses de Taizé, 1962. English ed., *Mary, Mother of the Lord, Figure of the Church,* Faith Press, London, 1963.

"L'unité visible," *Verbum Caro*, vol. 16(1962), pp. 150-160.

"Intercommunion," *ibid.*, vol. 17(1963), pp. 199-213.

Amour et vérité se rencontrent, Les Presses de Taizé, 1964.

"Une acte oecuménique du Concile: le vote de la Constitution dogmatique sur la révélation," *Verbum Caro*, vol. 19(1965), pp. 6-10.

INDEX OF NAMES

INDEX OF SUBJECT MATTER

and, 69; vocation to, 100, 119 ff., 143 ff.
Eschatological meaning, of celebacy, 73 ff.; of Church, 187
Eucharist, 9, 19; celebration of, 179 ff.
Evangelical counsels, viability, 1 f., 46 ff. *See also* Community of goods, Celibacy, Acceptance of authority.
Experimentation, 7, 9, 11 f., 28 ff., 100 f.

Faith, vocation and, 45 f.
Feasts, liturgical, 173
Flexibility, 10, 81, 85 f., 94, 134
Flowers, 173
Formalism, 176
Franciscans, 147 f., 187
Fraternities, 37 f., 151 ff., 165, 168
Freedom, celibacy and, 81

Gospel, reading of, 184; Rule and, 103 f., 110. *See also* Bible.
Group project, 86 f.

Hermitage, 103, 178
History, theology of, 17 ff.
Holy Spirit, guidance by, 43 ff.; perpetual vows and, 47 ff.
Hospitality, 143 ff.

Icon, 172
Idealism, 92
Improvisation, 155, 170 f.
Individual and community, 46, 80 ff., 84 ff., 119, 127
Individualism, 17 f., 23 ff., 55, 80 ff., 84, 91, 98, 167, 177, 182
Inspiration of founders, 109
Institutionalization,   108 ff., 129 f., 167, 174
Integralists, 133 f.
Intercommunion, 17, 181, 184
Involvement, 23 ff., 27, 38
Irresolution, 105 f.

Juridical aspect, of profession, 51 ff.; of religious life, 92, 94, 108 ff.; of ministry, 185 ff.

Lay aspect of religious, 35, 75
Love, celibacy and, 73 ff., 80 ff.; obedience and, 84

Marienschwestern, 13
Marriage, 46, 48, 68 ff., 111 f.
Meditation, 174
Methodism, 10 f.
Missions, ecumenism and, 17 f.; work of, 36 ff.
Mobility, 1, 12 f., 69, 81, 87, 100, 112, 113 ff.

Novitiate, training, 36, 110 ff.; second, 154

Obedience, 2. *See also* Acceptance of authority.
Office, 9, 145, 153 f., 165 ff.
Openness, 56, 97, 99, 113
Operation Hope, 159 ff.
Oxford Movement, 8 ff., 179

Paternalism, 90
Pelagianism, 52
Penance, sacrament of, 9, 19, 56 f.
Petrifaction, 1 f., 112, 142
Poverty, 54 ff. *See also* Community of goods.
Prayer, 8, 124, 149 f., 163 ff.; free, 169 f. *See also* Office.
Priesthood, universal, 181 ff.
Prior, function of, 89 ff.
Profession, religious, 47, 51 ff.
Progressives, 133 f.
Protestantism, ecumenism of, 17 ff.; solidarity, 131 f.
Providence, 44 ff.
Provisionality, 12, 113, 114, 186 f.

Reconciliation, 125 f., 137, 139
Reformation, community life and, 1 ff., 7 ff., 13 ff., 28
Relativity, of celibacy's motiva-